TOP **10**
SEATTLE

ERIC AMRINE

DK
EYEWITNESS TRAVEL

Contents

Left **Rachel the Pig, Pike Place Market** Center **EMP Museum** Right **Laguna pottery**

LONDON, NEW YORK,
MELBOURNE, MUNICH AND DELHI
www.dk.com

Printed and bound in China
First American Edition, 2005
16 17 18 10 9 8 7 6 5 4
Published in the United States
by DK Publishing,
345 Hudson Street
New York, New York 10014
**Reprinted with revisions 2007, 2009,
2011, 2013, 2015**
**Copyright 2005, 2015 © Dorling Kindersley
Limited, London**
A Penguin Random House Company

ISSN: 1479-344X
ISBN: 978-1-4654-2958-2

Within each Top 10 list in this book, no
hierarchy of quality or popularity is implied.
All 10 are, in the editor's opinion, of roughly
equal merit.

MIX
Paper from
responsible sources
FSC   FSC™ C018179
www.fsc.org

Contents

Seattle's Top 10

Pike Place Market	8
Seattle Center	10
Seattle Waterfront	12
Pioneer Square	14
International District	16
Broadway	18
Lake Washington Ship Canal	20
University of Washington	22
Woodland Park Zoo	24
Discovery Park	26
Moments in History	30
Architectural Highlights	32
Festivals & Parades	34
Museums	36
Performing Arts Venues	38
Children's Attractions	40
Seattle Pastimes	42

Contents

Left **Alki Beach** Right **University of Washington**

Getting Physical	44
Urban Retreats	46
Nightlife	48
Restaurants	50
Stores & Shopping Centers	52
The Eastside	54
Day Trips: Islands & Historic Towns	56
Day Trips: Mountain Getaways	58

Around Town

Downtown	62
Capitol Hill	70
Fremont	80
Ballard	88
West Seattle	96

Streetsmart

Planning Your Trip	104
Getting to Seattle	105
Getting Around Seattle	106
Things to Avoid	107
Budget Tips	108
Special Needs	109
Banking & Communications	110
Security & Health	111
Shopping Tips	112
Eating & Accommodation Tips	113
Places to Stay	114
General Index	120
Street Index	128

Left **Washington State Ferry on Puget Sound** Right **Seattle Art Museum**

Key to abbreviations
Adm *admission charge* **Free** *no admission charge* **Dis. access** *disabled access*

SEATTLE'S TOP 10

Seattle Highlights
6–7

Pike Place Market
8–9

Seattle Center
10–11

Seattle Waterfront
12–13

Pioneer Square
14–15

International District
16–17

Broadway
18–19

Lake Washington
Ship Canal
20–21

University of Washington
22–23

Woodland Park Zoo
24–25

Discovery Park
26–27

Top Ten of Everything
30–59

SEATTLE'S TOP 10

✓ = did it

⑩ Seattle Highlights

Seattle is a bustling powerhouse of influence, steering the future of high technology as well as popular culture. The population of this vibrant metropolis is fueled by espresso coffee, the latest developments in software, music, and visual art that's often as far on the leading edge as the city itself. Seattle has emerged as one of the most attractive cities in the United States, with an ever-changing skyline that reflects the pioneering spirit that brought settlers here in the mid-19th century.

1 Pike Place Market

An integral part of the Seattle experience, visitors flock to this thriving landmark all year round. Explore the invigorating mix of fresh seafood, farmers' produce, flower stalls, and ethnic foods *(see pp8–9).*

2 Seattle Center

The site of the 1962 World's Fair, the Seattle Center is now entirely dedicated to the pursuit of arts and entertainment. While many original edifices remain – the Space Needle being the most recognized – the location also inspires new building designs, such as Frank Gehry's EMP Museum *(see pp10–11).*

3 Seattle Waterfront

Seattle is a major port for both industrial and passenger traffic. Along with the Seattle Aquarium, sights include pier shops and restaurants just blocks from towering industrial cranes loading containers onto freighters *(see pp12–13).*

4 Pioneer Square

A treasure trove of Victorian-era architecture and streets still paved with bricks or cobblestone, Seattle's original commercial center was established in 1852 when Aurthur A. Denny and David Denny arrived with a handful of fellow pioneers. This is now a protected National Historic District *(see pp14–15).*

5 International District

The ID, as locals call it, is a mélange of Chinese, Korean, Japanese, and Southeast Asian cultures. Seattle's Pacific Rim identity makes it a final destination for émigrés from across the Pacific *(see pp16–17).*

Previous pages **Seattle skyline with Space Needle in the forefront**

Broadway 6

A summer night along Capitol Hill's main strip can resemble midtown Manhattan in terms of lively street scenes. Expect the unexpected – outrageous attire and flamboyant behavior *(see pp18–19)*.

Lake Washington Ship Canal 7

Officially completed in 1934, the Canal bisects the city and provides access to the sea for pleasure boaters, research vessels, and commercial barges alike *(see pp20–21)*.

University of Washington 8

One of the nation's top universities, UW comprises a student body of over 43,000, an attractive campus, and huge endowments from local benefactors in the high-tech industry *(see pp22–23)*.

Woodland Park Zoo 9

The design of Seattle's world-class zoo affords its animals vast enclosures. Natural habitats surround the viewing areas and pathways snake through its 92 acres (37 ha) *(see pp24–25)*.

Discovery Park 10

Rising above Puget Sound is a gorgeous 534-acre (216-ha) park. Densely wooded trails, beaches, historic military homes, and wildlife are just some of its attractive features *(see pp26–27)*.

TOP10 Pike Place Market

The Market stretches for several blocks high above the port traffic sailing on the gleaming waters of Elliott Bay. This historic district includes a meandering multi-level underground arcade, and street-level tables and stalls. Established in 1907, America's oldest continually operating farmers' market has become one of Seattle's most treasured institutions. By mid-century, most farmers' tables were run by Japanese-Americans, and their tragic internment during World War II nearly ended the market's operation. Plans to raze the old buildings fortunately ceased in 1971, when architect Victor Steinbrueck and his supporters saved them from the wrecking ball.

Neon fish advertisement

Famous neon cup sign

🍴 The market abounds in ethnic foods. Three Girls Bakery offers freshly baked bread and tasty sandwiches. For delicious in-door dining, head to Il Bistro for Italian, Place Pigalle for French urban, or Café Campagne for French country cuisine.

- Map J4
- Between Pike & Virginia St, from 1st to Western Ave; (206) 682-7453; www.pikeplacemarket.org
- Open daily except Thanksgiving, Christmas & New Year's Day.
- Three Girls Bakery: 1514 Pike St; (206) 622-1045
- DeLaurenti: 1435 1st Ave; 1-800-873-6685
- Café Campagne: 1600 Post alley; (206) 728-2233
- Il Bistro: 93a Pike St; (206) 682-3049
- Place Pigalle: 81 Pike St; (206) 624-1756

Top 10 Sights
1. Pike Place Fish Company
2. Starbucks
3. Victor Steinbrueck Park
4. Underground Mezzanines
5. Buskers
6. Farmers Market
7. DeLaurenti
8. Hillclimb
9. Hmong Flower Stalls
10. First and Pike News

Pike Place Fish Company
Crowds and film crews gather to witness these entertaining fishmongers *(right)*. Their skills include hurling fish high over customers and countertops to be weighed, filetted, and wrapped for travel.

Starbucks
The West was won with steamed milk and dark roast coffee. Howard Schultz's global retail coffee empire began right here in 1971, at Starbucks' first store *(above)*.

Victor Steinbrueck Park
Its wonderful grassy hill makes this a popular lunch destination. Pack a picnic, find a spot, and drink in the gorgeous views of Puget Sound, the Olympic Mountains, and Seattle's skyline.

Underground Mezzanines
Follow a maze of ramps and stairways to reach this shopping wonderland. Browse collectibles and books, have your palm read, commission a portrait, or treat yourself to local arts and crafts.

Summer Saturdays are the market's busiest days. For a more leisurely visit, try a weekday morning.

DeLaurenti

Step inside to sample the delicious offerings of this Mediterranean gourmet grocery. Fresh breads and cheese, and a large wine selection create a great summer picnic.

Buskers

Street music (*above*) is a constant feature of Market life. You might catch the hyperkinetic show of a spoons player who featured in at least one award-winning rock video, or be entertained by gospel quartets, piano troubadours, or a kazoo soloist.

Hmong Flower Stalls

Seattle's small, entrepreneurial SE Asian Hmong community dominates the Market's flower stalls. You can smell the blossoms from oversized bouquets even before seeing them through the crowds. In winter, residents make do with equally colorful dry flowers.

First and Pike News

This quaint, old-fashioned newsstand (*below*) offers a wide array of newspapers and magazines from around the world.

Hillclimb

This enclosed stairway and elevator connects the Market to the waterfront and more stores and restaurants in between. It also offers enchanting sea-to-mountain views (*below*).

Rachel the Pig

Don't miss Rachel, Seattle's largest piggy bank. This brassy icon of the Market Foundation also serves as the Market's sentry at the main entrance. All proceeds from visitors' donations to Rachel go towards low-income groups.

Farmers Market

Sample the produce of Washington's organic farmers at the popular outdoor Farmers Market (*above*), held on Fridays, Saturdays, and Sundays from June through September. The market is located between Pine Street and Stewart Street.

 Don't try driving through crowded Pike Place. Instead, use the parking lots on Western Avenue, then take a walking tour.

⭐ Seattle Center

The site of the 1962 Century 21 Exposition, tagged "America's Space Age World's Fair," Seattle Center has thrived through decades of massive growth all around it. The main attraction is still the Space Needle, though a close second is the ultra-modern and controversial EMP Museum, Paul Allen's monument to rock music. The International Fountain also attracts throngs of visitors. For the city's residents, Seattle Center is synonymous with lavish presentations of art, theater, dance, and music all year long.

EMP Museum

Space Needle, Seattle's iconic landmark

🍴 Center House contains many restaurants, but for a wider selection, including Thai restaurants, walk along Queen Anne Ave. For baked goods and espresso, try Uptown Espresso & Bakery, 525 Queen Anne Ave N; (206) 285-3757.

• Map H2 • Seattle Center: (206) 684-7200; www.seattlecenter.com • Space Needle: (206) 905-2100; www.space needle.com; 9am–midnight • McCaw Hall: (206) 733-9725; www.mccawhall.com • EMP Museum: (206) 770-2700; www.empmuseum.org • Monorail: (206) 905-2620; www.seattlemono rail.com • KeyArena: (206) 684-7200; www.keyarena.com • Pacific Science Center: 200 2nd Ave N; (206) 443-2001; www.pacificscience center.org • Seattle Children's Theatre: 201 Thomas St; (206) 441-3322; www.sct.org

Top 10 Sights

1. Space Needle
2. McCaw Hall
3. EMP Museum
4. Center House
5. Bagley Wright Theatre
6. Seattle Center Monorail
7. KeyArena
8. Bumbershoot
9. Pacific Science Center
10. Seattle Children's Theatre

1 Space Needle
This imposing structure *(see p32)* is recognized as the city's architectural icon. Ride the vintage external elevators to the 520-ft-(158-m-) high observation deck for a majestic view, or reserve a table at the revolving SkyCity restaurant for 360-degree panoramic views while dining.

International Fountain

2 McCaw Hall
The luxurious Marion Oliver McCaw Hall *(below & p38)* is home to the Seattle Opera and Pacific Northwest Ballet. The site also contains a café and the Boeing plaza.

3 EMP Museum
Paul Allen, co-founder of Microsoft and avid rock aficionado, commissioned distinguished modern architect Frank Gehry to design this technicolor exhibition space and performance venue *(see p32)*. It is also home to the Science Fiction Hall of Fame.

4 Center House
This large building houses the wonderful Seattle Children's Museum *(see p40)* as well as an intimate theater. It also contains restaurants, cafés, and shops.

Seattle Center used to be a favorite potlatch site for coastal Native Americans until the late 19th century.

5 Bagley Wright Theatre

The anchor for the Seattle Repertory Group, the theater rose in 1963 to become a Tony Award-winning playhouse. It is the largest of the three stages the Rep *(right & p38)* operates for its performances.

6 Seattle Center Monorail

Planners of the 1962 World's Fair imagined the future of mass transportation might resemble this train *(right & p32)*. The Monorail, still in operation today, makes the 1-mile (1.6-km) trip between Seattle Center and downtown every 10 minutes, daily.

7 KeyArena

The largest indoor venue *(below & p38)* in Seattle Center, with events ranging from heavy metal concerts to women's pro basketball games.

8 Bumbershoot

Seattleites mark their calendars for the long Labor Day holiday weekend in September, when Bumbershoot brings artists and imaginative literary arts programs, musicians, independent films, ethnic food, visual arts, and many surprises to Seattle Center for the region's largest festival of its kind *(see p34)*.

9 Pacific Science Center

You'll find exhibits on topics such as electronic music making, robotics, hydraulics, and natural history *(below)*. There's also a toddler area and two IMAX theaters.

10 Seattle Children's Theatre (SCT)

An award-winning organization that entertains 220,000 patrons each year. The Charlotte Martin Theatre and the Eve Alvord Theatre are recognized for innovative family-oriented programs.

1962 World's Fair

The Century 21 designers demonstrated their vision of the future in 1962, only 53 years after Seattle's first World's Fair, the Alaska-Yukon-Pacific Exposition. Modernity ruled, from the science-fictionesque Needle and Monorail to the Sputnik-like Center Fountain. Nearly 10 million visitors came to marvel at this ideal future. Even Elvis Presley made an appearance, filming *It Happened at the World's Fair* (1963). Today, it is considered strictly retro, if not kitsch.

Head to the International Fountain to watch the jets of water pulsing to music and to see kids of all ages getting wet!

10 Seattle Waterfront

One of Seattle's most distinguishing features is its working waterfront. It is the core of Seattle's thriving maritime community and is chock-full of the sights, shore-bird cries, and briny air of a seaport metropolis. It's the place to catch ferries to Bainbridge Island or the Kitsap Peninsula, or view sea life at the Seattle Aquarium. The piers are tourist central, replete with restaurants and bars, import shops, and harbor tours. Sculptures by well-known modern artists are on display at the Olympic Sculpture Park near the waterfront.

Seattle Aquarium

🍴 Catch your fresh seafood meal at Anthony's Pier 66 & Bell St Diner, 2201 Alaskan Way, (206) 448-6688, a respected Seattle institution. There's a carry-out section for fish 'n' chips or chowder, a seafood vendor, and an excellent indoor restaurant with dockside seating.

• Map H4
• Ferries Terminal: Pier 52; (206) 464-6400; www.wsdot.wa.gov
• Seattle Aquarium: Pier 59; (206) 386-4300; www.seattleaquarium. org; 9:30am–5pm daily; Adm • Ye Olde Curiosity Shop: Pier 54; (206) 682-5844; www.yeolde curiosityshop.com; summer: 9am–9:30pm; winter: 10am–6pm Sun–Thu, 9am–9pm Fri–Sat
• Tillicum Village, Blake Island: Pier 55; (206) 622-8687; www.tillicum village.com; departures Mar–May, Sep: 11:30am & 4:30pm Sat & Sun; Jun–Aug: 11:30am daily, 6:30pm Sat, 4:30pm Sun; Adm $79 adults, $72 seniors, $30 5–12 years (under-5s free)

Top 10 Sights

1 Seattle Great Wheel
2 Washington State Ferries
3 Seattle Aquarium
4 Ye Olde Curiosity Shop
5 Bell Harbor Marina
6 Water Sports & Tours
7 Tillicum Village, Blake Island
8 Myrtle Edwards Park
9 Cruise Ship Terminals
10 Olympic Sculpture Park

Seattle Great Wheel
1 For spectacular views of the city skyline, a 20-minute spin on Seattle's Great Wheel *(above)* is a must. The 175-ft- (53-m-) tall structure, with 42 fully enclosed gondolas, is perched dramatically over Elliott Bay.

Washington State Ferries
2 An icon of the Pacific Northwest, these ferries provide a picturesque, inexpensive cruise across Puget Sound, as well as transporting Seattle's commuters from neighboring shores.

Seattle Aquarium
3 The waterfront's most popular all-weather attraction is the world-class Seattle Aquarium. Make a point to step inside the Aquarium's glass-domed room *(below)* under 400,000 gallons of water for spectacular shark and octopus views. Watch divers feed the fish in the Underwater Dome and the sharks in the Pacific Coral Reef Exhibit. There are talks and crafts activities for children.

CityPass offers admission to multiple attractions such as Seattle Aquarium and Argosy Cruises: adult $64, child $44. See p108

Ye Olde Curiosity Shop
Looking for literature etched on rice grains, or other such unique objects? Since 1899, this has been the place *(above)* to find curios both from the distant and recent past. It's also a great source for coastal Native American art.

Seattle Waterfront

Pier 59
Pier 56
Pier 55
Pier 52/53

Cruise Ship Terminals
Seattle's relative proximity to Alaska's stunning Inside Passage, coupled with modern trends in leisure travel, led the city to build two terminals to accommodate the thousands of passengers coming and going. You can watch ships docking by the Bell Harbor Marina all summer long.

Bell Harbor Marina
This harbor *(above)* provides moorage for pleasure boats, large and small. It's adjacent to the port of Seattle's cruise-ship terminal.

Water Sports & Tours
If you're feeling adventurous, strap on a paraglider and head up for a breathtaking ride and aerial city view. Many boat cruises depart from here.

Tillicum Village, Blake Island
The 4-hour visit to this Native American cultural center begins with a 45-minute narrated cruise. You will be welcomed with steamed clams in broth, served salmon baked over an alder fire, and see a spectacular show of traditional dance, songs, and stories.

Myrtle Edwards Park
Visit this waterfront haven *(left)* for fine views of Mount Rainier, Puget Sound, and the Olympic Mountains. A bike trail and pedestrian path winds along the Elliott Bay coastline. The park also has a fishing pier.

Olympic Sculpture Park
Located at the southern end of Myrtle Edwards Park, this park showcases outdoor sculpture by Alexander Calder, Ellsworth Kelly, and many others. The views from the park are sensational.

Seafair & Tugboat Races
One of the most famed summer events is Seafair, a citywide festival that includes the famous tugboat races on Elliott Bay. Neither sleek nor sluggish, these champions of the sea are something to behold *(see p34)*.

For an unparalleled cityscape, catch a Washington State Ferry to Winslow on Bainbridge Island, returning to Seattle at sunset.

🔟 Pioneer Square

The birthplace of modern Seattle has a colorful history marked by economic and geological fluctuations. The Great Fire of 1889 virtually destroyed it, before Alaska's Gold Rush breathed new life and Victorian architecture into the mix. The old warehouses and narrow streets gave rise to a thriving loft arts scene in the 1980s and 1990s. While rents have skyrocketed and developers continue to renovate the grand facades of relic buildings, the galleries, cafés, and entrepreneurial spirit remain. The district stands as a testament to a city's survival, particularly after a devastating earthquake in 2001.

Cedar totem poles

🔵 If it's rainy or cold, curl up under Grand Central Bakery's cozy fireplace with a good book and a tasty treat.

• Map K5
• Seattle Metropolitan Police Museum: 317 3rd Ave S; (206) 748-9991; www.seametropolice museum.org; 11am–4pm Tue–Sun; Adm $4 adults, $2 under-12s
• Bill Speidel's Underground Tour: 608 1st Ave; (206) 682-4646; www. undergroundtour.com
• Grand Central Bakery: 214 1st Ave S; (206) 622-3644
• Merchant's Café and Saloon: 109 Yesler Way; (206) 467-5070
• Klondike Gold Rush National Historical Park: 319 2nd Ave S; (206) 220-4240

Top 10 Sights

1. Smith Tower
2. Metropolitan Police Museum
3. Bill Speidel's Underground Tour
4. First Thursdays
5. Pioneer Square
6. Grand Central Bakery
7. Waterfall Garden
8. Merchant's Café and Saloon
9. Klondike Gold Rush National Historical Park
10. Skid Road

Smith Tower
Built in 1914 by type-writer tycoon L.C. Smith, at 42 stories this skyscraper *(above & p33)* was once the tallest edifice west of New York. Ride the hand-operated elevator to the observation deck for great views.

② Seattle Metropolitan Police Museum
Police artifacts dating from the 1880s, including weapons, uniforms and photographs, are on display at this intriguing museum. Visitors can learn about some of Seattle's notorious crime cases and even sit in a jail cell.

③ Bill Speidel's Underground Tour
Deliberately unusual in name and nature, this outfit presents a remarkable look at Pioneer Square's underground history. The Great Fire, tidal patterns, and poor sewage design forced citizens to convert second stories into first, shown through this subterranean 90-minute walk starting from Pioneer Building *(below & p33)*.

First Thursdays

On the first Thursday of each month, from noon to 8pm, galleries sponsor a well-attended art walk. Patrons can talk directly to the artists about their displayed works. An ideal starting point is Occidental Way between Main and Jackson Street, where you can find many of the galleries *(right)* and upscale shops.

Klondike Gold Rush National Historical Park

A versatile display of exhibits, films, and photographs emphasize Seattle's role as the closest US city to Alaskan gold, and as a crucial supply post for claim stakers *(below & p30)*.

Skid Road

Henry Yesler's logging mill sat at the foot of what is now Yesler Way, a hill as long and steep as any in San Francisco. He used it to slide timber down to the wharf. When Pioneer Square's economy tumbled, Skid Road came to signify desolation and despair.

Pioneer Square

This cobblestone triangle of land bordered by Yesler Way and First Avenue is notable for a Tlingit totem pole, and a statue of Seattle's namesake, Chief Sealth. The square also features an iron-and-glass pergola *(above)* built in 1909 that once marked the entrance to the "finest underground restroom in the United States."

Waterfall Garden

In the Northwest, water is everywhere. Step inside this tiny private park to meditate on a man-made paean to tumbling water *(below)*.

Grand Central Bakery

This is the artisanal bakery and café that helped make hand-rolled European-style bread a mainstay in Seattle.

Merchant's Café and Saloon

Popular and prospering since 1890, Seattle's oldest restaurant dishes up hearty meals amid Victorian decor.

Nisqually Earthquake

In February 2001, Pioneer Square and the entire Puget Sound region experienced a 40-second earthquake, measuring a whopping 6.8 on the Richter scale. Several otherwise sturdy and fireproof brick-and-mortar constructions from post-1889 met their match. Falling bricks and facades crushed cars and damaged many edifices *(see p31)*.

Make a day out of touring both Pioneer Square and the ID (see pp16–17); bus 99 links these adjacent districts.

ⁱ⁰10 International District

Once known as Chinatown, this district was renamed when community leaders recognized that inhabitants from all over Asia had made that term obsolete. One of Seattle's most historical districts, the ID is a striking example of how Asian cultures thrive and assimilate into Western society. Each ethnicity claims a particular quadrant, even while coexisting in the same colorful part of town. Stroll through groceries and restaurants run by Cambodians, Koreans, Japanese, Vietnamese, and others, to experience the Orient, Pacific Northwest style.

Dragon depicting Asian culture

Chinese dipping sauce

🍜 For tasty Vietnamese, try Thanh Vi at 1046 S Jackson St, (206) 329-0208. For Chinese, head to Seven Stars Pepper Szechuan Restaurant at 1207 S Jackson St, Suite 211, (206) 568-6446.

- Map L6
- ID: (206) 382-1197; www.cidbia.org
- Union Station: 401 S Jackson St; (206) 398-5000 • Jade Garden: 424 7th Ave S; (206) 622-8181 • Harbor City Restaurant: 707 S King St; (206) 621-2228
- Wing Luke Museum: 719 S King St; (206) 623-5124; www.wingluke.org
- Tsue Chong Co. Inc.: 800 Weller St S; (206) 623-0801; 9:30am–5pm Mon–Fri, 10:30am–2pm Sat
- Seattle's Best Tea: 506 S King St; (206) 749-9855
- Uwajimaya: 600 5th Ave S; (206) 624-6248
- Safeco Field: (206) 346-4000 • CenturyLink Field: (206) 381-7555
- Great Wall Mall: 18230 E Valley Hwy, Kent; (425) 251-1600; 9am–9pm daily

Top 10 Sights

1. Chinese Lunar New Year
2. Little Saigon
3. Union Station
4. Dim Sum
5. Wing Luke Museum
6. Tsue Chong Co. Inc.
7. Seattle's Best Tea
8. Uwajimaya
9. Train Tunnel
10. Safeco/CenturyLink Field

1 Chinese Lunar New Year

A traditional celebration in Chinese communities worldwide, Seattle's version takes place inside the Great Hall of the historic Union Station. Streetside Kung Fu lion dances *(right)*, music, and firework displays make this a festive day for both locals and tourists looking for winter fun in the city.

2 Little Saigon

The storefronts here resemble images of 1960s-era Saigon, with large, bright signage in the native language *(below)*.

3 Union Station

This Beaux Arts-style station *(above)* opened in 1911 with a black-and-white mosaic floor and a 55-ft (16-m) vaulted ceiling that supports hundreds of lights. It has been sensationally remodeled and is now popular as an event venue.

Avoid parking in the ID on game days at Safeco or CenturyLink Fields or you'll be fighting crowds on the streets and sidewalks.

Dim Sum
Seattleites are serious about their food, and flock to the International District for these mandatory Chinese delicacies *(above)*. Excellent choices are Jade Garden and Harbor City Restaurant.

Tsue Chong Co. Inc.
If you smell something sweet amid pungent aromas of the International District, it's likely to be this outfit, which makes delicious noodles and fortune cookies.

Seattle's Best Tea
Tea finds its rightful place in a city overrun by coffee shops. Joe Hsu's small, bright, modern shop is the real deal. Customers can sample the delicious teas. Prices range from $20 to $217 per pound.

Train Tunnel
Passenger and freight trains thunder below the edge of the ID. The tunnel ends just past Pike Place Market.

Wing Luke Museum
The vision of civic leader Wing Luke who died in a plane crash in 1965, this museum explores the culture and history of Asian Pacific Americans through a series of permanent and visiting exhibitions *(see p37)*.

Uwajimaya
If you can't make it to the Far East, head to the largest Asian market in the Pacific Northwest *(below)*. This store has a vast array of Asian products, merchandise, and a huge ethnic food court offering cuisine from all over Asia.

Safeco Field/ CenturyLink Field
Seattle's professional baseball and football teams are based across the street from each other, in the space between International District and Pioneer Square *(above)*.

Great Wall Mall
This 9-acre (3.6-ha) mall offers an amazing Asian shopping extravaganza. It's a bit of a drive to the east of Sea-Tac Airport, but the sheer size and selection of these Asian import stores is worth seeing. Retailers here mirror the local immigrant populations and influences not only from China, but also from all over Asia.

Broadway

This is the main drag that slices across Capitol Hill, one of Seattle's edgier communities just up the hill from downtown. Hip stores and a wide variety of cafés and restaurants attract a thriving gay culture and gritty youth population. On warm nights, Broadway is about as urban as Seattle gets, as it surges with pedestrians. Thanks to the avenue's proclivity for over-the-edge fashion, people-watching can be a great source of entertainment. Sleek new condos, retail space, and a light-rail station (opening 2016) to connect Capitol Hill with downtown and the University District are changing the face of Broadway.

Jimi Hendrix Sculpture

This cast-iron sculpture of rock legend Jimi Hendrix is located by the popular Pike/Pine corridor.

Broadway Performance Hall, Capitol Hill

🕐 There are several pockets of panhandlers and homeless street people along Broadway. Use your discretion if asked for donations.

- Map L3
- Broadway Performance Hall: 1625 Broadway; (206) 325-3113
- Cal Anderson Park: 11th between Pine St E/ Denny Way E
- Red Light: 312 Broadway Ave E; (206) 329-2200; www.redlightvintage.com
- Quest Bookshop: 717 Broadway Ave E; (206) 323-4281
- Mishu Boutique: 321 Broadway Ave E; (206) 802-8022; www.mishuboutique.com
- The Vajra: 518 Broadway Ave E; (206) 323-7846
- Dick's Drive-In: 115 Broadway Ave E; (206) 323-1300

Top 10 Sights

1. Broadway Performance Hall
2. Jimi Hendrix Sculpture
3. Cal Anderson Park
4. Dance Steps on Broadway
5. Red Light
6. Quest Bookshop
7. Mishu Boutique
8. The Vajra
9. Harvard Exit/Egyptian Theaters
10. Dick's Drive-In

Broadway Performance Hall

Originally Broadway High School, the hall *(see p39)* is part of the campus for Seattle Central Community College. Victor Steinbrueck was instrumental in restoring this structure. Its repertoire includes film festivals, and music and dance recitals.

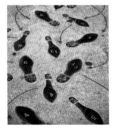

Water sculpture, Cal Anderson Park

Cal Anderson Park

Named after one of Washington's openly gay legislators, the park features Lincoln Reservoir, Bobby Morris Playfield, tennis courts, a children's play area to the southeast, and an interactive water feature.

Dance Steps on Broadway

Sculptor Jack Mackie created an amusing series of inlaid bronze dance steps *(left)* along the sidewalks of Broadway in 1982.

Parking on Capitol Hill is at a premium; leave the car at the hotel and take a bus or taxi instead.

5 Red Light
This two-story bastion of quirk and fashion is Seattle's largest vintage clothing store *(right)*. Choose from a varied collection with the help of friendly and informed staff.

6 Quest Bookshop
With extremely knowledgeable and helpful staff, this cozy bookstore *(see p76)* offers a huge range of writings on world religions and spiritual traditions. You'll also find a good selection of such things as crystals and Tibetan singing bowls.

9 Harvard Exit/Egyptian Theatres
Broadway's two vintage movie houses *(below & p39)* showcase independent films from directors on the vanguard. The Seattle International Film Festival *(see p35)* makes liberal use of both the theaters each year.

10 Dick's Drive-In
Seattle's homegrown version of a fast-food hamburger joint, and unadulterated Americana to boot since 1954, this branch is a magnet for crowds on weekend nights. Quick and delicious, but not recommended for cholesterol-watchers.

8 The Vajra
The name translates as "Destroyer of Ignorance", and this shop is perfect for your Tibetan Buddhist meditation supplies. Look for block-print tapestries, scented oils, and incense. It's also a popular spot for tarot card reading *(below)*.

7 Mishu Boutique
Located in the artists' haven, Fremont, Mishu *(above)* leads the market in modern and trendy outfits for young fashionistas. The clothing and jewelry is designed locally and handmade in India.

KING < CUPS

Pill Hill

An affectionate term for First Hill, the area almost indistinct from Capitol Hill along the same high ridge above downtown. It's thick with most of the area's hospitals and medical research facilities, hence the nickname.

Lake Washington Ship Canal

What began in Montlake as a tiny log flume is now an 8-mile (13-km) urban waterway for sailboats, kayakers, and an impressive fleet of industrial vessels heading to sea. In 1854, pioneer Thomas Mercer recognized the need for a passage to the ocean from Seattle's two landlocked water bodies, Lake Washington and Lake Union, to replace the cumbersome transport of natural resources such as coal and timber. The Ship Canal and the Locks were completed in 1917 by the US Army Corps of Engineers. Four drawbridges cross the Canal at strategic points in Ballard, Fremont, the University District, and Montlake, at the western edge of Lake Washington.

Kayaks

🌀 If you plan on kayaking, be wary of weather changes any time of year, as winds can pick up and severely affect current and surface water conditions. Look out for larger ships that may sneak up unknowingly on smaller craft.

• Map E2
• Hiram Chittenden Locks: 3015 NW 54th St; (206) 783-7059; Grounds: open 7am–9pm daily; Visitor Center: open May–Sep: 10am–6pm daily, Oct–Apr: 10am–4pm Thu–Mon

Top 10 Sights

1. Making the Cut
2. Bascule Bridges
3. Montlake
4. Lake Union
5. Working Waterfront
6. Christmas Ships
7. *Sleepless in Seattle*
8. Urban Wildlife
9. The Locks
10. Shilshole Bay

Making the Cut
Retired US Army Corps of Engineers general, Hiram M. Chittenden lobbied Congress to fund the initial earth-moving in 1911. Part of the Canal's construction necessitated lowering Lake Washington's water level by 9 ft (3 m).

Bascule Bridges
These bridges operate with counterweights and cantilevered sections that can be raised and lowered. Fremont and Ballard bridges are the oldest, built in 1917. The former is only 30 ft (9 m) above the waterline, and opens about 35 times each day *(below)*.

Montlake
At the base of Capitol Hill's northeastern tip, the upmarket community of Montlake abuts the Arboretum and the Ship Canal. Just across the Canal, the university's huge Husky Stadium *(above & p23)* dominates the majestic view.

Lake Union
A very urban lake with Seattle's downtown skyline framing its southern shore *(above)*. Seattle's maritime museum, Center for Wooden Boats *(see p37)* and Lake Union Park at the south end are worth a visit.

Urban Wildlife
Although the Ship Canal is literally and figuratively far from any wilderness, it still attracts diverse wildlife. Blue heron, gulls, beaver, Canada geese, and migrating salmon are among the many creatures to look for.

The Locks
Officially completed in 1917, the Hiram M. Chittenden Locks link the Sound and Salmon Bay at Ballard *(left)*. About 100,000 vessels pass through annually, as do salmon runs in the adjacent fish ladder – fully equipped with observation windows for visitors.

Shilshole Bay
The western terminus of the Ship Canal feeds into this scenic bay, home to a public marina. The waterfront boasts fine seafood restaurants, meeting spaces, and Golden Gardens *(see p47)* park.

Working Waterfront
Seattle's maritime industry prospers along the Ship Canal route. Tanker ships or gill netters lie in dry dock, boat dealers proliferate, and oil booms float here and there – in stark contrast to the natural ecology that struggles to survive.

Sleepless in Seattle
The idiosyncratic floating home enclaves *(below)* of northern Lake Union and Portage Bay are visible almost exclusively by boats traveling the Canal and environs. One was a focal point in the Meg Ryan and Tom Hanks romantic film, *Sleepless in Seattle* (1993).

Christmas Ships
Every December, local boaters celebrate the holiday season by venturing out during several cold evenings after decorating their boats with creative and colorful light displays.

Opening Day Events

Seattleites take water and boating very seriously, but anyone can sail the waterways. The official boating season begins the first Saturday in May, with a series of waterborne celebrations sponsored by the Seattle Yacht Club. Constant drawbridge openings snarl traffic for the Parade and Regatta, as the region's small ships fill the Ship Canal and adjacent lakes with revelers and those captains who may have waited all winter to sail.

The Locks have been designated a National Historic Place. They are still operated by the US Army Corps of Engineers.

10 University of Washington

Founded in November 1861, just 10 years after the creation of Washington Territory, the prestigious UW moved to its present location with 639 hilly acres (258 ha) in 1895. It was also the site of the festival grounds for Seattle's Alaska-Yukon-Pacific Exposition in 1909. Supporting a 43,000-member student body that's as eclectic as the architectural mix on campus, the institution has garnered a reputation internationally for its undergraduate and postgraduate curricula in biomedical research, public health, law, computer science, and oceanography. Wide-open quads, cherry blossoms in spring, and lovely views provide a relaxing counterpoint to the buzz of advanced learning.

University campus

🍴 There's no shortage of eateries on "The Ave". For pub grub and the best microbrew in the U District, try Big Time Brewery & Alehouse (206-545-4509).

Nothing beats drinks, lunch, or dinner at Agua Verde Café and Paddle Club (206-545-8570). Get there early to avoid the lines. Rent kayaks bound for Lakes Washington and Union, via the Ship Canal.

• Map E2
• UW: (206) 543-9198; www.washington.edu
• Henry Art Gallery: (206) 543-2280; www.henryart.org • Meany Theatre: 4001 University Way NE; (206) 543-4880; www.meany.org • Burke Museum: (206) 543-5590; www.burkemuseum.org
• University Book Store: 4326 University Way NE; (206) 634-3400; 9am–8pm Mon–Fri, 10am–7pm Sat, noon–5pm Sun

Top 10 Sights

1. The Hub
2. Red Square
3. Henry Art Gallery
4. Husky Stadium
5. Paul G. Allen Center for Computer Science & Engineering
6. Meany Theatre
7. Suzzallo Library
8. Burke Museum
9. Medicinal Herb Garden
10. University Book Store

University of Washington

1 The Hub
The main student union building is known as "The Hub" *(above)* due to its central position on campus. It's information central, as well as a venue for visiting performers.

2 Red Square
Named for the inlaid brick pavers underfoot, the huge Square lies between Meany Theatre, Kane Hall, and the Suzzallo Library. It's also known for hosting impromptu midnight concerts by musicians seeking free expression.

3 Henry Art Gallery
Founded in 1927, this was the first public art gallery *(below & p36)* in Washington, which quadrupled its size in 1997 to make room for larger, adventurous, modern exhibits and collections and to enhance collaborative educational programs. It also has a bookstore and a café.

A walk around the university campus is definitely a worthwhile experience, especially during spring.

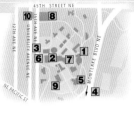

4 Husky Stadium
At the base of Capitol Hill's northeastern community of Montlake abuts the Arboretum and the Ship Canal (see pp20–21). Just across the Canal, the university's huge Husky Stadium, the home of the top-rated UW Huskies, dominates the view.

5 Paul G. Allen Center for Computer Science & Engineering
This $72-million facility was named after one of the two founders of Microsoft.

9 Medicinal Herb Garden
Escape for a captivating spell on 2 acres (1 ha) of land (below) where several hundred species flourish and herbal scents abound. It also features a Drug Plant Garden planted in 1911.

10 University Book Store
The main branch of the bookstore rivals the best in independent and larger chain book vendors for sheer selection and informed staff.

6 Meany Theatre
The shining glory of professional performance arts on campus, the theater hosts performers of all disciplines from all over the globe. It also supports the school's drama, music, dance, and experimental digital media curricula.

7 Suzzallo Library
Once known as "the soul of the University," the library is the crowning glory of the Neo-Gothic style on campus. The astounding vaulted ceiling rises 65 ft (20 m) above the second floor reading room. It also offers classes on research and technology skills.

8 Burke Museum
The state's official museum (below) for natural and cultural history is a jewel of the campus. Large collections of Pacific Rim and Northwest Native American cultural heritage items are on display. The museum also organizes specialized tours and a summer discovery camp for children.

The Ave
The main commercial artery serving the U District is University Way NE, called "The Ave," which is all about youth culture. It's lined with coffee shops, music stores, clothiers, as well as bookstores that have lasted generations, and restaurants serving reasonably priced food from every culture imaginable. In 2003, in a grand effort to beautify the street, the city widened sidewalks, and enhanced law enforcement, adding some sparkle to what had been suffering neglect for years.

ᵀᴼᴾ10 Woodland Park Zoo

Designed in 1909 by architect John Olmsted, this is one of the oldest zoos on the West Coast. Occupying an area of 92 acres (37 ha), the landscape offers a natural habitat for nearly 300 animal species. Reflecting a naturalistic mission to advocate conservation and education while imparting the value of an ecological perspective, the animal habitats are as close to nature as possible. African mammals roam grasslands of a savanna; African and Asian elephants thrive in Thai-style setting; grizzly bears frolic over logs and in a stream running down a steep hill. Popular with families of young children is the petting zoo, literally a hands-on activity that's fun and educational.

Main entrance gate to Woodland Park Zoo

🍴 **Inside the West Gate are several places to eat in the Pavilion, where you'll find the Market Grill, Sabino's Specialties, Wok in the Wild, and other food counters.**

🕐 **You can visit Woodland Park across Hwy 99 (Aurora Avenue) from the zoo.**

- Map D1
- Woodland Park Zoo: 601 North 59th St; (206) 548-2500; www.zoo.org; May–Sep: 9:30am–6pm daily; Oct–Apr: 9:30am–4pm daily; Adm: adults $18.75 May–Sep, $12.75 Oct–Apr; children (3–12) $11.75 May–Sep, $8.75 Oct–Apr; toddlers (0–2) free

Top 10 Sights

1. Jaguar
2. Gorillas
3. Elephant Forest
4. African Savanna
5. Nocturnals
6. Birds of Prey
7. Northern Trail
8. Orangutans/Siamangs
9. Komodo Dragons
10. Plants & Pathways

1 Jaguar
The largest cat species in the Western Hemisphere and an endangered species *(above)*. The habitat features a cave, a pool for his swimming preferences, and jungle-like terrain that brings the fearsome animal close enough to touch save for the glass enclosure.

2 Gorillas
In one of the most cherished spots at the zoo you can view two multigenerational gorilla families, cavorting only inches away on the other side of the glass.

3 Elephant Forest
View zookeepers groom and feed the elephants *(below)* several times a day. There are also scheduled demonstrations of elephants performing tasks such as log stacking.

Gardeners reserve their cherished spot each year when zoo officials unload prized composted animal manure – "Zoo Doo".

4 African Savanna

Lions, giraffes, hippos, spotted hyenas, gazelles, wild dogs, white-faced whistling duck, patas monkey, zebras, and Egyptian geese make this city-bound safari one of the largest and most exhilarating places *(below)*. Observe from an overlook dedicated to guitarist and Seattle native Jimi Hendrix.

7 Northern Trail

This is where to find the deceptively playful-looking grizzly bears *(above)*. Nearby, packs of gray or timber wolves seem haunted, and the extremely threatened river otters dive underwater and resurface with total abandon.

9 Komodo Dragons

The world's largest carnivorous lizards *(below)* can weigh as much as 500 pounds (226 kg) with a length of 9 ft (3 m), and are excellent swimmers. Not recommended for pets, but great for the imagination.

10 Plants & Pathways

Take the time to appreciate the careful consideration zoo landscapers have given to this human environment. The shrubbery *(below)* is lush and plentiful, and lends an exotic ambience to the occasion.

5 Nocturnals

Take a break from the screech and howls of outdoor wildlife for the dark and silent mysteries of nocturnal creatures. Watch boas, pythons, vampire bats, tomato frogs, blue-tongued skinks, and much more.

6 Birds of Prey

Watch falconers send regal winged predators out and back by the Raptor Center. Perched on fence posts, owls *(right)* and red-tailed hawks may reside calmly in full panoramic view.

8 Orangutans/ Siamangs

With intelligence that approaches our own, orangutans are still hilarious to observe. Also view siamangs, native to the island of Sumatra and the Malay Peninsula.

ZooTunes Summer Concerts

The zoo departs from its main agenda every summer with one of Seattle's musical highlights. Residents from the surrounding neighborhood and all over town meet on the North Meadow in the late afternoons and early evenings for a picnic dinner, and take in entertainment from some of the best known musicians worldwide. In keeping with the zoo's family theme, children under 12 are admitted free.

 Look out for the iridescent tail feathers of resident peacocks who wander the walkways and surprise onlookers.

⁷₁₀ Discovery Park

Occupying the northwestern edge of the Magnolia headland north of Elliott Bay, Discovery Park is Seattle's largest and most varied in-city escape. Even though the US Army's Fort Lawton sold surplus base territory to the city, Army Reserves still use a portion of the park for training and officers' quarters. At 534 acres (216 ha), the park consists of densely wooded rainforests crisscrossed with trails, high bluffs of eroding sand at the edge of a huge meadow, and 2 miles (3 km) of driftwood-laden beaches on Puget Sound, providing a real sense of wildness.

A beach at Discovery Park

🕙 Plan an itinerary in advance based on the amount of time you have to spare. There are no concessions in the park, so bring snacks or a picnic lunch with you.

• Map A2
• Discovery Park: 3801 Discovery Park Blvd; (206) 386-4236; www.seattle.gov; 4am–11:30pm daily; Visitors' Center: 8:30am–5pm Tue-Sun
• Daybreak Star Indian Cultural Center: (206) 285-4425; www. unitedindians.com

Top 10 Sights

1. Bluff Trail
2. Military Residences
3. Daybreak Star Indian Cultural Center
4. West Point Lighthouse
5. Beach Walks at Low Tide
6. Loop Trail
7. Eagle-Watching
8. Playgrounds
9. West Point Treatment Plant
10. Go Fly a Kite

Bluff Trail
The trail leads from the South Gate along a meadow's edge to the majestic overlook with breathtaking views of the Olympic Mountains and Puget Sound.

Military Residences
The park is dotted with clusters of abandoned and still-in-use Army base housing, listed on the National Register of Historic Places. Most are off-limits to visitors, but you can get a closer look at them near the former parade grounds.

Daybreak Star Indian Cultural Center
Operated by the United Indians of All Tribes Foundation, the center houses a collection of Native American art. There's an arts and crafts gallery, traditional salmon bakes, and an annual summer powwow celebration *(below)* on the grounds of Discovery Park.

West Point Lighthouse
As picturesque as can be, the lighthouse *(below)* shines light through the fog from its perch on a narrow spit of land jutting out into the water. Feel free to stroll up to and around the automated sentinel, even though it's not open for touring.

Stay off the sandy, constantly eroding bluffs. Rangers periodically relocate the Bluff Trail to prevent accidents.

Beach Walks at Low Tide

Seattleites escaping the hustle and bustle of the city come to walk along the waterfront parks around the Sound. The beach at Discovery Park is a preferred spot for those in the know.

Playgrounds

For an outing with children, head for the small playground behind park headquarters at the east entrance. Or, ask for one of only five parking passes available for families with young children so you can drive directly down to the alluring shore of Discovery Park.

Go Fly a Kite

The hilly field between the main bluffs and a radar ball behind barbed wire makes for some of the best kite flying (above) in town, as updrafts from the sea seem almost constant throughout the year.

Loop Trail

Stroll along the trail that brings you through the varied terrain of Discovery Park. Explore the easy route to find overgrown rainforest ravines, flowering meadowlands, creeks, thickets, streams, sand dunes, and blackberry brambles galore.

West Point Treatment Plant

An extraordinary reminder of the city outside, this facility is so exquisitely landscaped to be almost invisible from hiking trails. This ultramodern wastewater treatment plant is as environmentally conscious as technology allows.

Eagle-Watching

Occasionally, bald eagles (right) nest in the highest treetops in Discovery Park, home to more than 250 species of birds and other wildlife. You may find park volunteers surrounded by eager bird-watchers with binoculars. Chances are, they have sighted a nest.

Sharing the Land

In many ways, land use at Discovery Park represents the harmonious balance between natural conservation and urban development, and a coexistence of US military and Native American tribes. In 1970, a group of protesters led by activist Bernie Whitebear staged an invasion and occupation of the still-active military base, in part to establish a cultural land foundation for urban Indians. After an exhausting three months for both sides, and many arrests, Whitebear's group acquired a 99-year lease for 20 acres (8 ha) of parkland.

 Following pages **West Point Lighthouse at Discovery Park**

Left **Asian settlers, West Seattle** Right **Klondike Gold Rush National Historical Park**

Top 10 Moments in History

Native American Roots
Archaeological records date the first inhabitants of the Seattle region to 11,000–12,000 years ago. Tribes included the Suquamish, Duwamish, Nisqually, Snoqualmie, and Muckleshoot, who, despite their harsh environment, evolved into complex societies that traded with other tribes.

Denny Party
In 1851, Chief Sealth of the Duwamish Tribe greeted Arthur A. Denny and his group of European settlers at West Seattle's Alki Point *(see p97)*. Subsequently, Denny served as a delegate to the Monticello convention, which gave rise to the states of Oregon and Washington.

Northern Pacific Railroad
Seattle's neighbor, Tacoma, was the original terminus of 1873's Northern Pacific Railroad, linking the region to the rest of the country. By 1893, another transcontinental railroad, the Great Northern Railway, extended into Seattle, eventually supplanting Tacoma as the Puget Sound region's main rail depot.

Lumber Mills
When timber baron Frederick Weyerhaeuser purchased nearly a million acres of railroad land in 1900, Seattle's mushrooming logging industry turned a corner for even more rapid growth and exploitation of natural resources. Until then, entrepreneurs such as Henry Yesler ruled the wharf, and erected the pioneer town out of lumber from ancient old growth forests.

Great Fire of 1889
Natural resources created a boomtown whose rapid growth drew more than 1,000 new residents every month. Seattleites learned the impermanence of wooden structures in 1889, after a catastrophic fire destroyed much of the downtown area.

Arthur A. Denny

Klondike Gold Rush
The Alaska Gold Rush *(see p15)* officially kicked off in 1897 after a gold-filled steamship docked at Seattle's waterfront. As the last gas for prospectors and suppliers bound for the gold fields, this city prospered as never before.

Boeing's Beginnings
Recognizing the need for airplanes as the United States entered World War I in 1917, William E. Boeing hired pilot Herb Munter to design a seaplane for the Navy. The rest of the giant Boeing Corporation's success is history.

Devastation after the 2001 earthquake

Rise of Microsoft

8 In 1975, Harvard dropout Bill Gates and his high-school friend Paul Allen founded Microsoft. From the suburb of Redmond, they launched a personal computer revolution and have never looked back. Today, Microsoft's Windows operating system is the dominant computer platform, and the company employs more than 78,000 people worldwide.

Nisqually Earthquake

9 If Seattle is a boom and bust town, it certainly felt the boom in a magnitude-6.8 earthquake on the morning of February 28, 2001 *(see p15)*. Workers escaped their offices, if they could, to see the earth rolling, pavements cracking, and cars violently swaying. The region suffered more than $1 billion in damages.

Green River Killer Caught

10 The Seattle area lived under a dark shadow of brutal serial killings as dozens of women became victims of the Green River Killer. Twenty years of intense investigation led to the capture of Gary Ridgway in 2001. He was convicted in 2003.

Top 10 Famous Seattleites

1 **Chief Sealth (1786–1866)**
Seattle draws its name from the Duwamish leader.

2 **John Nordstrom (1871–1963)**
Originally a shoe seller, the Nordstrom family empire is now a chain of upscale department stores.

3 **Eddie Bauer (1899–1986)**
The inventor of the goose-down parka opened his first store of clothes and sporting goods in Seattle.

4 **Bruce Lee (1940–1973)**
This Kung-Fu legend and movie star lived in Seattle.

5 **Jimi Hendrix (1942–1970)**
A self-taught electric guitarist and legend, Hendrix continues to influence today's music with his original compositions.

6 **Ted Bundy (1946–1989)**
The serial killer of the 1980s admitted to 30 murders and was executed in 1989.

7 **Howard Schultz (b. 1953)**
Schultz turned a few local coffee stores into the global Starbucks empire worth billions of dollars.

8 **Bill Gates (b. 1955)**
Co-founder and now technology advisor of Microsoft, he is one of the world's richest men.

9 **Jeff Bezos (b. 1964)**
This Internet billionaire founded giant web retailer Amazon.com in 1995.

10 **Gary Locke (b. 1950)**
The first Chinese-American governor in US history, Locke also served as Secretary of Commerce from 2009 to 2011.

Left **EMP Museum** Center **Pioneer Building** Right **Metro Bus Tunnel**

🔟 Architectural Highlights

Space Needle
Seattle's modern architectural identity began with the Space Needle *(see p10)*, designed by John Graham and Company, for the 1962 World's Fair. The three pairs of beams supporting the spire lie buried 30 ft (8 m) underground, and have secured the 605-ft (185-m) Needle during several earthquakes and gale-force windstorms. ◈ *Map H2*

EMP Museum
Designed by renowned Post-Modern architect, Frank Gehry, this technicolor facility *(see p10)* resembles a smashed guitar, in homage to Jimi Hendrix's incendiary finales. Paul Allen's provocative project emphasizes Seattle's role as the artistic and musical vanguard. ◈ *Map H2 • 325 5th Ave N • www.empmuseum.org*

Central Library
Award-winning Dutch architect Rem Koolhaas designed the $196.4-million insulated glass and steel structure to replace Seattle's vintage 1960 Central Library. The unusual oblique structure and

Central Library

glass flooring have been controversial, but defenders of the building insist that, once inside, people will love it *(see p64)*. ◈ *Map K5 • 1000 4th Ave • www.spl.org*

Columbia Center
This 76-story skyscraper rises high above any other Seattle structure. Completed in 1985, from a design by Chester Lindsey Architects, it is currently the second-tallest building west of the Mississippi River. Three of the 46 elevators bring visitors to the posh private club at the top. It offers stunning views of Elliott Bay, the Olympic Peninsula, Mount Rainier, and the Cascade Mountains. ◈ *Map K5 • 701 5th Ave • (206) 386-5564 • Observation deck: 9am–10pm daily • Adm for observation deck*

Seattle Center Monorail
One of the city's favorite attractions is the Monorail, an exciting two-minute ride *(see pp11 & 64)* designed by Alweg Rapid Transit Systems. Each year, 1.5 million passengers board its original 1962 cars to get a taste of what designers imagined at the time would be the mass transit model of the future. The Monorail connects downtown with the Seattle Center and departures are every 10 minutes from Westlake Center (5th & Pine St) and the Seattle Center station (across from the Space Needle). ◈ *Map H2 • Seattle Center • (206) 905-2620 • 7:30am–11pm Mon–Fri, 8:30am–11pm Sat & Sun • Adm • www.seattlemonorail.com*

Rainier Tower

Designed by renowned Japanese architect Minoru Yamasaki in 1977, this unique 40-story structure resembles an upside-down skyscraper, as its main tower rises from a relatively narrow 11-story pedestal. Rainier Square *(see p53)*, an upscale underground shopping mall, occupies much of its ground level. ✪ Map K4 • 1301 5th Ave

Brass elevator doors of the 1914 Smith Tower

Seattle Tower

This charming Art Deco building was designed by architects Albertson, Wilson & Richardson in 1929. The facade's tan brick and multiple shades of granite set it apart from its steel and glass neighbors. Vertical accents make its 27 stories appear even taller, and the lobby's ornate bronze and marble detail is capped by a fanciful ceiling bas-relief depicting local flora and fauna.
✪ Map K4 • 1218 3rd Ave

Smith Tower

Typewriter tycoon L.C. Smith erected Seattle's first skyscraper *(see p14)* in 1914. The white terracotta building has brass hand-operated elevators that take visitors to the Chinese Room at the 35th level, with its antique carvings and inlaid porcelain ceiling, and an observation deck.
✪ Map K5 • 506 2nd Ave
• Adm for observation deck
• www.smithtower.com

Pioneer Building

This striking 1892 building of red brick and terra-cotta, designed by Elmer H. Fisher, boasts a National Historic Landmark status. During the Gold Rush years, 48 mining outfits maintained offices here, and it became headquarters for a prosperous speakeasy during Prohibition. Bill Speidel's Underground Tour *(see p14)* starts here. ✪ Map K5 • 608 1st Ave

Downtown Seattle Transit Tunnel (DSTT)

From the Washington State Convention Center to the International District, this tunnel was designed to carry riders aboard buses that switch from diesel to electric energy while underground. Between 2005 and 2007 the tunnel was retrofitted to accommodate a light-rail service that began operating in 2009, linking downtown Seattle with Seattle–Tacoma International Airport (Sea–Tac). ✪ Map K3

Left **Seafair** Right **Bumbershoot**

Festivals & Parades

1 Seafair
A parade along 4th Avenue in late July is a highlight of Seafair, a celebration of maritime and aviation history highlighted by the aerodynamic "derring-do" of the Navy's Blue Angels F/A-18 fighter pilots, an All Nations Pow Wow at Daybreak Cultural Center, hydroplane races on Lake Washington, and battleships open to the public on the waterfront.

Crowds watching the Blue Angels, Seafair

2 Bumbershoot
Performers from all over the world converge for this Labor Day weekend festival *(see p11)* that transforms Seattle Center into the arts capital of the Pacific NW. Its three days are packed with concerts, intimate theater productions, independent film presentations, and literary arts.

3 Seattle Pride March
The Seattle Pride March *(see p72)* runs from Westlake Park to Seattle Center. Sponsored by the gay, lesbian, bisexual, and transgender community, it attracts huge crowds from every orientation. Expect outrageous floats, dancing, and the popular "Dykes on Bikes", a motorcycle outfit whose members freely show what they have beneath the leather.

4 University District StreetFair
Dating from 1970, Seattle's first street fair stretches over ten blocks of "The Ave" and its side-streets in May. Innumerable crafts booths, food vendors, and local rock music performances attract families from all over town.

5 Fremont Fair Solstice Parade
All floats at this innovative parade must be entirely human powered, stimulating the imaginations of Fremont's anarchic arts community. Crews propel samba bands, dancers, and rock quartets using battery-operated amplifiers. It's held on or near the summer solstice (June 21).

6 Seattle Maritime Festival
Aficionados of tugboats and ships flock to this May festival. It makes for a free, fun, and family-friendly way to learn how the working waterfront has become a major factor in Seattle's economy and culture. The fair centers around the Bell Street Pier, which is a short walk north from the Seattle Aquarium on Pier 62 *(see p12)*. An exciting and humorous highlight is the tugboat race on Elliott Bay.

For more information on Seattle Pride March, held in late June each year, visit www.seattlepride.org

7 Northwest Folklife Festival

A free Memorial Day weekend celebration of the Pacific NW's ethnic music, dance, and arts and crafts, Folklife is a magnet for all the old (and new) hippies in the region.

Rainbow Lady, Folklife Festival

Given the diversity of Seattle's Pacific Rim population, it's virtually a festival of and for the world.

8 Seattle International Film Festival (SIFF)

One of the most respected and comprehensive film festivals in the US, SIFF screens more than 400 new works from at least 60 countries during May and June. Even midnight showings of cult films sell out, and notable directors attend many premier screenings.

9 Earshot Jazz Festival

The shoestring staff at the non-profit Earshot Jazz held between October and November present a well-respected event. The festivals have consistently showcased successful as well as emerging jazz artists, enriching and enlightening the Seattle community at large. Well-known performers have included Bill Frisell and John McLaughlin.

10 Seattle Improvised Music Festival (SIMF)

The largest and longest running music festival of its kind anywhere, SIMF is dedicated to the esoteric art of spontaneous composition. Local performers join eclectic international musicians to improvise sets that defy category, but always impress. After 27 thrilling annual productions, the ever-popular February festival draws larger audiences each year.

Top 10 Festál Cultural Events

1 Tết Festival
A colorful beginning in late January marks the Vietnamese Lunar New Year.

2 Irish Week Festival
Music and dance events comprise two days of authentic Irish culture in mid-March.

3 Seattle Cherry Blossom & Japanese Cultural Festival
Dance, music, martial arts, and tea ceremonies are the highlights of this mid-April fair.

4 Festival Sundiata
Seattle's celebration of the West African Mansa of the Mali Empire, in June, represents African and African-American cultural traditions.

5 Pagdiriwang Philippine Festival
Philippine independence is marked in mid-June with dance, film, drama, and culinary arts.

6 BrasilFest
Expect infectious rhythms, joyful dance, and spicy flavors to celebrate this Brazilian Folklore Day in late August.

7 TibetFest
This late-August festival preserves Tibet's rituals and traditions while incorporating cultural elements of its neighboring countries.

8 Festa Italiana
This late September festival is all about Italian style fun and food.

9 Día de Muertos
Pay tribute to your ancestors Latin American-style with altars, artwork, food, and music in early November.

10 Hmong New Year
November marks the end of harvest, a time for relaxing and preparing special foods.

Left **Seattle Art Museum** Center **Frye Art Museum** Right **Henry Art Gallery**

Museums

1 Seattle Art Museum

Jonathan Borofsky's 48-ft- (15-m-) tall, black metal *Hammering Man* stands outside Seattle's largest art museum *(see p63)*. SAM's permanent collection includes European, Asian, African, and Northwest Coast Native American works. ◎ Map J4
• 1300 First Ave • (206) 654-3100 • Open 10am–5pm Wed–Sun (to 9pm Thu) • Adm (free 1st Thu of month) • www.seattleartmuseum.org

Hammering Man

2 Seattle Asian Art Museum

The historic 1933 Art-Moderne structure in Volunteer Park houses Seattle Art Museum's Asian art collection, primarily works from China, Japan, and Korea.
◎ Map E4 • 1400 E Prospect St • (206) 654-3100 • Open 10am–5pm Wed–Sun (to 9pm Thu) • Adm (free 1st Thu of month) • www.seattleartmuseum.org

3 Frye Art Museum

Wealthy industrialists Emma and Charles Frye's collection of 19th- to 20th-century representational art is on view at this elegant

Seattle Asian Art Museum

gallery. Exhibits include works by American masters such as Mary Cassatt, Winslow Homer, John Singer Sargent, and Andrew Wyeth. ◎ Map L4
• 704 Terry Ave • (206) 622-9250 • Open 11am–5pm Tue–Sun (to 7pm Thu) • Adm • www.fryemuseum.org

4 Museum of History & Industry

Located in Lake Union Park, this is a gem for anyone interested in the region's work and workers over the last 150 years. Key features include photographs and a rich catalog of oral histories. ◎ Map K1 • 860 Terry Ave N • (206) 324-1126 • Open 10am–5pm daily (to 8pm Thu) • Adm (free 1st Thu of month) • www.mohai.org

5 Henry Art Gallery

This modern art museum *(see p22)* at UW presents work by cutting-edge artists. It also offers imaginative programs and exhibits, and promotes experimental art by encouraging dialogue on contemporary culture, politics, and aesthetics. ◎ Map E2
• NE 41st St & 15th Ave NE • (206) 543-2280 • Open 11am–4pm Wed, Sat, & Sun, 11am–9pm Thu & Fri • Adm (Thu is "pay what you wish") • www.henryart.org

6 Burke Museum

Founded in 1885, the Burke is a natural history buff's dream. View dinosaur and dragonfly fossils, hand-carved Native American cedar canoes, and interesting gems and minerals.

*Map E2 • NE 45 St & 17th Ave NE
• (206) 543-5590 • Open 10am–5pm daily
(to 8pm 1st Thu of month) • Adm (free 1st
Thu of month) • www.burkemuseum.org*

7 Northwest African American Museum

Here you can trace the history and traditions of African-Americans in the Pacific Northwest, from slavery to the present day. *Map E6 • 2300 S Massachusetts St • (206) 518-6000 • Open 11am–7pm Tue, 11am–4:30pm Wed, Fri, & Sat, noon–4pm Sun • Adm (free 1st & 2nd Thu of month) • www.naamnw.org*

8 Museum of Flight

Walk through a model of the Space Shuttle, tour the first Air Force One, designed for President Kennedy, climb into the cockpit of a mint-condition SR-71 Blackbird or F/A-18 Hornet fighter jet, or step aboard a Concorde *(see p41)*. *Map P2 • 9404 E Marginal Way S • (206) 764-5720 • Open 10am–5pm daily (to 9pm 1st Thu of month) • Adm • www.museumofflight.org*

9 Center for Wooden Boats

CWB has over 100 small vessels and offers classes in maritime activities and crafts. During their annual July festival, you can tour relic sloops and tugs. For an in-city adventure, try sailing one of the historic boats. *Map D4 • 1010 Valley St • (206) 382-2628 • Open 10am–8pm Tue–Sun (to 5pm in winter) • www.cwb.org*

10 Wing Luke Museum

Named after a civic leader who lobbied for Asian-American rights, this museum fulfills Wing's dream to showcase the culture and history of Asian immigrants. *Map L6 • 719 S King St • (206) 623-5124 • Open 10am–5pm Tue–Sun (to 8pm on free days) • Adm (free 1st Thu & 3rd Sat of month) • www.wingluke.org*

Top 10 Northwest Artists

1 Jacob Lawrence (1917–2000)
Lawrence established a national reputation as a painter and activist.

2 Mark Tobey (1890–1976)
A 1953 *Life* magazine featured Tobey as one of the four "Mystic Painters of the Pacific Northwest." He was a major influence on Jackson Pollock.

3 George Tsutakawa (1910–1997)
He gained international fame as a painter, sculptor, and fountain-maker.

4 Morris Graves (1910–2001)
This Northwest painter continues to inspire Seattle artists.

5 Paul Horiuchi (1906–1999)
His heavily textured, abstract Expressionism collage painting utilized Zen philosophy to create mysterious works.

6 Guy Anderson (1906–1998)
Part of the 1953 *Life* feature, Anderson led an eccentric but influential life as a painter.

7 Kenneth Callahan (1905–1986)
Another artist in the *Life* feature, he was once a curator at Seattle Art Museum.

8 Tony Angell (b. 1940)
A naturalistic painter, sculptor, and writer.

9 Dale Chihuly (b. 1941)
Chihuly's handblown decorative glass art has popularized the medium.

10 Clayton James (b. 1918)
James has painted landscapes, made furniture, and sculpted in multiple media.

Left **Benaroya Hall** Center **Moore Theatre sign** Right **Bagley Wright Theatre**

Performing Arts Venues

Benaroya Hall
This bastion of culture is the city's first venue designed exclusively for music performances. It is also home to the Seattle Symphony. The 2,500-seat Mark Taper auditorium is known for its superior acoustics. Another 540-seat hall is used for smaller concerts. ⊗ Map K4
• 200 University St • (206) 215-4747
• www.seattlesymphony.org

McCaw Hall
In 2003 the original opera house underwent a massive transformation to become McCaw Hall *(see p10)*. Built for no less than $127 million, this plush 2,900-seat auditorium with state-of-the-art acoustics and excellent amenities is home to the Seattle Opera and Pacific Northwest Ballet. ⊗ Map H1

KeyArena
The largest indoor venue *(see p11)* in Seattle Center is home to the city's professional women's basketball team, the Seattle Storm, and is a popular venue for major events and concerts. ⊗ Map G2

KeyArena

Paramount Theatre
One of the most treasured theaters in town, the faithfully restored Paramount dates from 1928 and exudes the charm of the popular Beaux-Arts style of grand movie palaces of its period. Today, it presents Broadway shows, jazz and rock concerts, and dance performances.
⊗ Map K3 • 911 Pine St • (206) 682-1414
• www.stgpresents.org

Moore Theatre
Built in 1907, the grand lobby and halls of Seattle's oldest theater flow with mosaic, stained glass, and woodcarvings. In 1974, it was placed on the National Register of Historic Places. It also serves as a base for new rock bands. ⊗ Map J4 • 1932 2nd Ave
• (206) 682-1414 • www.stgpresents.org

5th Avenue Theatre
Opening in 1926 as a vaudeville venue, 5th Avenue's ornate imperial Chinese design was inspired by Beijing's Forbidden City. It is Seattle's premier home for nationally touring musical theater. ⊗ Map K4
• 1308 5th Ave • (206) 625-1900
• www.5thavenuetheatre.org

Bagley Wright Theatre
The Bagley Wright Hall *(see p11)* at the Seattle Center belongs to the nonprofit Seattle Repertory Theatre, and is the flagship of the company's three performance venues. The Rep won the 1990 Tony Award for

Broadway Performance Hall

Outstanding Regional Theater, confirming its reputation for producing classic and contemporary plays of high literary standards. ✎ Map H1• 155 Mercer St • (877) 900-9285 • www.seattlerep.org

ACT Theatre/ Kreielsheimer Place
Housed in the beautifully refurbished Kreielsheimer Place (formerly Eagles Auditorium), the long-running A Contemporary Theatre showcases contemporary playwrights. Inside, the cultural center contains four performance spaces, ACT's administrative offices, rehearsal spaces, and scene and costume shops. ✎ Map K4 • 700 Union St • (206) 292-7676 • www.acttheatre.org

Broadway Performance Hall
Victor Steinbrueck, who helped preserve Pike Place Market (see pp8–9), was also instrumental in saving this auditorium (see p18) from the wrecking ball. Its repertoire includes film festivals, music and dance recitals, and off-the-wall theater. ✎ Map L3 • 1625 Broadway

Sky Church
EMP Museum's performance venue (see p10) is a 85-ft- (26-m-) high room, the ultimate facility for a band looking to use 48,000 watts of surround-sound amplification, exceptional computer-controlled light systems, and the world's largest indoor video screen. ✎ Map H2 • 325 5th Ave N • (877) 367-7361 • www.empmuseum.org

Top 10 Best Cinemas

1 Egyptian
With its kitschy decor the theater housed SIFF in the 1980s. ✎ Map L3 • 805 E Pine St • (206) 781-5755

2 Harvard Exit
Seattle's first art movie house. ✎ Map M2 • 807 E Roy St • (206) 781-5755

3 NW Film Forum
Has an independent cinema and studio for incubating new work. ✎ Map M3 • 1515 12th Ave E • (206) 329-2629

4 Cinerama
Paul Allen financed the restoration of this 808-seat movie house. ✎ Map J3 • 2100 4th Ave • (206) 448-6680

5 Fremont Outdoor Cinema (Summers)
A favorite for cult and classic movies. ✎ Map D2 • N 35th & Phinney Ave N • (206) 781-4230

6 Grand Illusion
They show the best of independent and avant-garde films. ✎ Map E2 • 1403 NE 50th St • (206) 523-3935

7 Rendezvous Cafe/ Jewel Box
This Belltown bar seats only a few die-hard fans of independent film. ✎ Map J3 • 2322 2nd Ave • (206) 441-5823

8 Majestic Bay
Ballard's vintage theater offers modern luxuries. ✎ Map B1 • 2044 NW Market St • (206) 781-2229

9 Neptune
Built in 1921 with a nautical motif and movie-palace grandeur. ✎ Map E2 • 1303 NE 45th St • (206) 781-5755

10 Varsity
The Varsity has thrived since it opened in 1940. ✎ Map E2 • 4329 University Way NE • (206) 781-5755

Left **Children's Museum** Center **Children's entertainment** Right **Northwest Puppet Center**

Children's Attractions

Children's Museum
In the heart of Seattle Center, this museum contains imaginative galleries and hands-on studio spaces that endlessly stimulate children's imaginations. The Global Village reveals lifestyles of Japan, Ghana and the Philippines, and the Bijou Theatre invites young performers to dress up and act out scripts provided by the museum. ✎ Map H2 • 305 Harrison St • (260) 441-1768 • Adm • www.thechildrensmuseum.org

International Fountain
During any festival and all through summer, the fountain draws hundreds of frolicking children. Weather permitting, kids strip down and dodge dozens of majestic arcs of water projecting out and up from the spherical base, all in time to music.
✎ Map H2 • 305 Harrison St • (206) 684-7200

International Fountain

Kids' Bookstores & Galleries
Seattle's many venues and activities designed for children include the excellent Secret Garden bookstore and the children's art gallery "Early Masters", which runs classes. ✎ Early Masters: Map E1; 8815 Roosevelt Way NE; (206) 274-1531 • Secret Garden: Map B1; 2214 NW Market St; (206) 789-5006

Toy Stores
The city's most popular local toy stores have a loyal following because their toys spur children's imaginations without sparing the fun. Browse the jam-packed aisles at Top Ten Toys and Magic Mouse Toys. ✎ Top Ten Toys: Map P2; 104 N 85th St; (206) 782-0098 • Magic Mouse Toys: Map K5; 603 1st Ave; (206) 682-8097

Children's Film Festival Seattle
This 10-day event gives young people and families the chance to enjoy and even judge new feature films. It is held annually from January to February.
✎ Map M3 • 1515 12th Ave • (206) 829-7863 • Adm • www.nwfilmforum.org

Northwest Puppet Center
Founded by the dedicated Carter Family Marionettes in 1986, this center offers a museum, archive and library, and over 250 annual performances. The troupe tours and also sponsors educational outreach programs worldwide. ✎ Map P2 • 9123 15th Ave NE • (206) 523-2579 • www.nwpuppet.org

Museum of Flight

Space Needle
A 41-second glass-elevator ride rockets you up to the observation deck for unforgettable views. But kids will probably remember best the Lunar Orbiter dessert served in the revolving SkyCity restaurant – an over-the-top ice-cream sundae, swathed in clouds of dry ice. It's truly out of this world *(see p10)*.

Museum of Flight
Many children wish to fly, or fly off the handle. Either way, one way to encourage the former and stifle the latter is to take them to this museum *(see p37)*. It also provides insightful outreach programs for school groups, families, and teachers.

Ride the Ducks
If you can't decide between a tour by land or sea, these amphibious vehicles from World War II make for an offbeat excursion around the waters of Seattle. Areas include downtown, the Pike Place Market, Pioneer Square, Fremont, and Lake Union's houseboats. ◊ *Map H2 • 516 Broad St • (800) 817-1116*

Tillicum Village
Blake Island, across the bay from the waterfront, contains a rainforest park and a fabricated Northwest Coastal Native American Village. A 4-hour adventure includes the cruise, traditional food, music, and dance, and time to stroll beaches and forested trails *(see p12–13)*.

Top 10 Hotels with Swimming Pools

Warwick Seattle Hotel
This Belltown hotel's many 24-hour extras and the pool make it even more family-friendly *(see p118)*.

Seattle Marriott Waterfront
This attractive waterfront hotel offers a heated indoor as well as outdoor pool, with views of Puget Sound *(see p114)*.

Marriott Courtyard
Relax in the hot tub while the kids frolic in the indoor pool. ◊ *Map D4 • 925 Westlake Ave N • (206) 213-0100*

Sheraton Seattle
Parents may prefer idle moments in the wine bar called the Daily Grill, but the hotel also has a heated indoor pool for all ages *(see p114)*.

The Westin Seattle Hotel
The indoor pool is an all-weather plus *(see p114)*.

University Inn
Families appreciate the inn's 100-percent non-smoking rule and free breakfast *(see p116)*.

Travelodge Seattle Center
Amenities are few, but there is a children's play area, free breakfast, and an outdoor pool *(see p118)*.

Fairmont Olympic Hotel
The indoor pool is just one of many amenities for those with deep pockets *(see p114)*.

The Maxwell Hotel Seattle
Conveniently located, dog-friendly hotel with a pool and free parking *(see p118)*.

Silver Cloud Inn
Take advantage of this inn's pool, complimentary breakfasts, and shuttles to downtown *(see p116)*

Left **Visitors at Green Lake** Right **Boaters on Green Lake**

Seattle Pastimes

Coffee Town
Seattle's signature beverage comes in myriad forms. The rampant availability of whole bean, latte, espresso, and basic drip created a coffee craze even before Starbucks went global. Though Seattleites love their streetside espresso carts and neighborhood cafés, the city is also home to the ubiquitous Starbucks and its major caffeinated competitor, Tully's.

Cold coffee

Gardening
Gardeners take advantage of the weather to grow astounding varieties of plants and trees that thrive in the mist and drizzle. Despite the short growing season, there's enough sunshine to keep urban pea patches and botanical gardens as thick and green as the rainforests are tall.

Kites at Gas Works Park
A favorite gathering spot is a hill overlooking Lake Union at Gas Works Park *(see p46)*. The wind patterns at this point attract kite flyers of all ages.

Public Art
Public art seems to grow like weeds, particularly in Fremont *(see pp80–83)*. Even bus tours cruise by the incongruous collection here – dinosaur topiaries, a Volkswagen-crushing troll under a highway, and a statue of Lenin, from the former Soviet Union. Other installations include *Waiting for the Interurban*, depicting bored commuters.

Code Warriors
Microsoft, its supporting vendors, and upstart competitors still employ thousands of computer programmers and developers. Writing the killer application inspires many an entrepreneur. The laptop user at the café table next to yours may well be the next software mogul.

Green Lake Jogs
Green Lake *(see p46)* attracts health- and nature-conscious visitors from around the city. A verdant setting and wide 2.8-mile (4.5-km) path encircling the lake attracts walkers, runners, bikers, and babystroller-pushing parents come rain or shine.

Kite flying at Gas Works Park

Readings & Lectures

Many authors make their home here, and historical fiction, music biography, and science fiction are just a few popular genres that have taken root. Capitol Hill's Elliott Bay Book Company (see p76) sponsors one of the region's most treasured reading and lecture series.

Historic Preservation

Seattle maintains a vital link to its past through architecture, due to the remarkable success of its preservationists. Pike Place Market (see pp8–9) is one shining example, and several downtown theaters and 19th-century structures in Pioneer Square (see pp14–15) have achieved landmark status. Seattle neighborhoods reveal several restored Craftsman-style homes.

Boating

An aerial view of Seattle reveals that this town practically floats in a vast watershed. Natural and man-made canals, rivers, lakes, and estuaries abound. Pleasure boats and commercial ships of all kinds ply the waterways of one of the busiest and most picturesque maritime communities in the United States.

Civil Unrest

When the WTO met in Seattle in 1999, thousands of demonstrators turned the city upside down. But that was only one chapter in a long history of civil disobedience. In the early 20th century, the International Workers of the World unionized logging and mining industries. Violent riots erupted in 1916 in Everett and in 1919 in Centralia, cities to the north and south of Seattle.

Top 10 Cafés

1 Café Besalu
This European-style café lures foodies with gourmet pastries. ◈ Map B1 • 5909 24th Ave NW • (206) 789-1463

2 Bauhaus Books & Coffee
(See p75).

3 Caffé Ladro
This local chain captures the basic espresso requirements: consistent pours and loyal clientele. ◈ Map E4 • 435 15th Ave E • (206) 267-0551

4 Zeitgeist
They make exceptional espresso and also sponsor art shows. ◈ Map K6 • 171 S Jackson • (206) 583-0497

5 The Elliott Bay Book Company & Café
(See p76).

6 Fremont Coffee Company
The coffee is superb, and there are also tasty wraps. ◈ Map D2 • 459 N 36th • (206) 632-3633

7 Lighthouse Roasters
They make rich drinks from freshly roasted coffee beans. ◈ Map D2 • 400 N 43rd • (206) 634-3140

8 Café Allegro
Keeps students, professors, and locals stoked on caffeine brewed to perfection. ◈ Map E2 • 4214 University Way NE • (206) 633-3030

9 Herkimer Coffee
A tastefully designed café in the quiet Greenwood neighborhood has a faithful following seven days a week. ◈ Map P2 • 7320 Greenwood N • (206) 784-0202

10 Tea House Kuan Yin
Offers fine teas and an ambience that's more Zen than zippy. ◈ Map D2 • 1911 N 45th • (206) 632-2055

Left **Sea kayaks, Lake Union** Right **A cyclist on Alki Beach**

Getting Physical

Climbing Rock Walls
The most popular indoor location for rock climbers is Recreational Equipment Incorporated (REI, *see p45*), which has a huge practice wall in the atrium of their flagship store on Eastlake Avenue. Stone Gardens also offers classes and practice walls for members and walk-ins. ◈ *Stone Gardens: Map B1 • 2839 NW Market • (206) 781-9828 • Adult $16; youth $11; under-15 $10; rental equipment extra • www.stonegardens.com*

Kayaking
Lake Union is the most convenient point, being so close to downtown and its Ship Canal links to Lake Washington and Shilshole. When there's no wind, the currents are barely an issue even for novices. More adventurous river-runners find their rapid transit in challenging whitewater courses closer to the mountains.

Skiing & Snowboarding
Seattleites wait anxiously for the first large snowfall that carpets ski runs in the Cascades. Crystal Mountain, Alpental,

Rock-climbing walls, Stone Gardens

Snoqualmie Pass, and Stevens Pass attract faithful downhill and cross-country skiers, and boarders who have honed their skills on the area's famously challenging snow conditions.

Burke-Gilman Trail
The legacy of two of Seattle's earliest railroad men, Judge Thomas Burke and Daniel Gilman, this disused railroad track is a paved trail *(see p84)* that stretches for about 27 miles (43 km) from the western edge of Ballard to the north end of Lake Washington. Cyclists and pedestrians can enjoy the scenic beauty of key sights such as Gas Works Park *(see p46)* and Magnuson Park at Sand Point.

Colman Pool
An alternative to the cold, inhospitable Puget Sound is a dip in Colman Pool. It uses heated and filtered saltwater drawn from Puget Sound, which it overlooks from its beach location within Lincoln Park *(see p47)*. ◈ *Map P2 • 8603 Fauntleroy Way SW • Open late May–Aug • Adult $4.75; child/senior $3.25*

Highland Ice Arena
There's only one year-round ice rink that serves Seattle. Loyal patrons include graceful figure skaters, daredevil hockey players, and novices young and old just starting to learn the ropes. ◈ *Map P2 • 18005 Aurora Ave N • (206) 546-2431 • Adult/teen (13–64) $7; child/senior (6–12/65+) $6 • www.highlandice.com*

If you bike the Burke-Gilman Trail, pay attention to the posted speed limits and keep right at all times.

7 Snowshoe Treks

One of the most popular wintertime sports is snowshoeing, an ancient method of walking on or through the white stuff. The National Park Service and local outfitters offer a series of guided walks. Beginners should start with an experienced professional guide to lead the outing.

8 Scuba Diving

For an adventurous sport opt for scuba diving in Puget Sound to discover undersea creatures such as wolf eels, octopus, sea stars, and urchins with amazing ranges of size and color. Divers embark solo or as part of chartered excursions to take advantage of the coastline that's never victim to heavy damage or dangerous currents from Pacific Ocean storms.

9 Windsurfing

For one of the country's premier windsurfing meccas, you'll have to go to Hood River, Oregon, in the Columbia River Gorge. If extreme sports are not your style, Seattle has two prime locations for all who want to let the wind sweep them away - along the west shores of Lake Washington, between Magnuson Beach and Seward Park; and at Golden Gardens Park, where Shilshole Bay meets Puget Sound.

10 Tolt-MacDonald Park & Campground

Many of Seattle's in-city parks have decent single tracks for casual mountain biking. But, for intermediate-level cyclists looking for small challenges in a great riverside setting, head 28 miles (45 km) east across Lake Washington to Carnation, in the Snoqualmie River valley.
🔅 Map Q2 • 31020 NE 40th St, Carnation

Top 10 Places to Rent Gear

1 REI

This store helped define Seattle as an outdoor recreation mecca. 🔅 Map K2 • 222 Yale Ave N • (206) 223-1944

2 Second Ascent

Rents snowshoes, trekking poles, helmets, plastic boots, ice axes, and crampons. (see p91) 🔅 Map B2 • 5209 Ballard Ave NW • (206) 545-8810

3 Feathered Friends

Has a great selection of climbing gear. 🔅 Map K2 • 119 Yale Ave N • (206) 292-2210

4 Agua Verde Café & Paddle Club

Rent a kayak or dine on great Mexican food. 🔅 Map E2 • 1303 NE Boat St • (206) 545-8570

5 Moss Bay Rowing & Kayaking Center

Offers a variety of kayaks and rowboats. 🔅 Map K1 • 1001 Fairview Ave N • (206) 682-2031

6 Gregg's Greenlake Cycles

Hire road bikes here. 🔅 Map E1 • 7007 Woodlawn Ave NE • (206) 523-1822

7 Greenlake Boat Rentals

Stand up paddle boats for rent. 🔅 Map E1 • 7351 East Green Lake Dr N • (206) 527-0171

8 Windworks Sailing Center

Rent bareboats, or take sailing lessons. 🔅 Map A1 • 7001 Seaview Ave NW • (206) 784-9386

9 Northwest Outdoor Center

Rent kayaks or paddle along the Canal. 🔅 Map D3 • 2100 Westlake Ave N • (206) 281-9694

10 Center for Wooden Boats

(See p37).

Free maps of cycling routes are available at the city's Bicycle and Pedestrian Program: 600 4th Avenue, (206) 684-7583.

Left **Gas Works Park** Right **Woodland Park Rose Garden**

Urban Retreats

Green Lake
The well-worn paths in this lake's *(see p42)* sylvan setting take visitors around a placid lake in a quiet neighborhood north of downtown. Mirror-smooth or gently rippling with the wind, Green Lake's mesmerizing surface lets minds wander freely. It's packed on weekends, especially in the summer months, when sunbathers flock to the grassy areas for day-long solar treatments. ◎ *Map D1*

Volunteer Park
Between 1904 and 1909, the Olmsted Brothers turned these 45 acres (18 ha) of hilltop into a bucolic grass meadow with a fantastic view. The park now houses the Seattle Asian Art Museum *(see p36)*, the Volunteer Park Conservatory, and an observation tower *(see p72)*. It's also a notorious gay pick-up scene at night. ◎ *Map E3 • 1247 15th Ave E*

Volunteer Park Conservatory

Gas Works Park
Set up in 1906 as a gasification plant to light the streets of Seattle, this became the first industrial site in the world to be re-created into a public park. The park has been scrubbed several times over the years, much of the oversized, industrial machinery either remains on exhibit, or sits rusted and threatening like industrial mastodons behind high-security fences. It has a high, grassy kite hill – topped with a sculptor's sundial. ◎ *Map D3*
• *2101 N Northlake Way • (206) 684-4075*

Woodland Park Rose Garden
New visitors to the Woodland Park Zoo *(see pp24–5)* often bump into this gated area near one of the Zoo entrances. Others, nearly a quarter million annually, make sure to wake up and smell the roses. About 5,000 individual plants and 280 varieties of rose turn this 2.5-acre (1-ha) corner of north Seattle into a technicolor dream. ◎ *Map D1*

Schmitz Preserve Park
The scant remains of the temperate rainforest old growth trees give a clue of what Seattle must have resembled before European settlement. Schmitz is essentially a deep, wide, heavily wooded ravine surrounded by residential streets, but street noises disappear among the magnificent trees and native plantlife. ◎ *Map A5 • (206) 684-4075*

For safety reasons, Seattle parks close by 10pm or 11pm, and it's best not to visit them after dark.

6 Washington Park Arboretum & Japanese Garden

Stroll the Washington Park Arboretum's 230 acres (93 ha) of carefully cultivated landscapes and rare tree species. The gardens, a living page of Japanese history, were built in 1960 according to plans by Japanese designer Juki Iida. These include a traditional sculpture, a stream, exotic flora, ponds, and a teahouse. ✪ Map F3 • 2300 Arboretum Dr. E • Japanese Garden: 1075 Lake Washington Blvd E • Adm

7 Seattle Chinese Garden

Discover one of the largest Chinese gardens outside of China at the South Seattle Community College campus. Built by artisans from Seattle's sister city, Chongqing, it spans two separate cultures. The Sichuan-style garden integrates China's history, art and architecture, philosophy, and literature. During major works over the next few years, guided tours are available. ✪ Map P3 • 6000 16th Ave SW • (206) 934-5219 • Adm

8 Center for Urban Horticulture

The University of Washington established the CUH in 1980 in order to exert more control and achieve sounder management of

Golden Gardens

the Arboretum. It includes a library, a herb garden, pleasant strolling meadows, and weekly master-gardener meetings. ✪ Map F2 • 3501 NE 41st St

9 Golden Gardens

In Ballard's far northwestern edge along Puget Sound, the wide sandy beaches of Golden Gardens (see p90) take on the characteristics of a cherished vacation spot. The Olympic Mountains stand to the west, a marina lies adjacent, and Lake Washington Ship Canal is nearby, so pleasure crafts are always in view. There are two wetlands, a wooded area, a stream, and a loop trail. ✪ Map P2

10 Lincoln Park

On the road to West Seattle's Fauntleroy Ferry Terminal (see p97), this is a versatile recreational find for those looking for hilly trails, picnics by the water, or even a dip in Colman Pool (see p44). ✪ Map P2

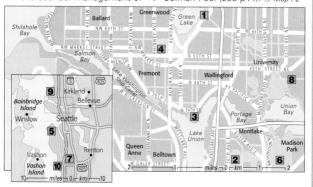

The Showbox

10 Nightlife

1 The Showbox

This elegant 1900s Art Deco room with state-of-the-art audio and computer-controlled lighting has been used as a concert hall, a comedy club, and even a rental space for a Talmud Torah Hebrew Academy Bingo series. Artists as dissimilar as Al Jolson, the Mills Brothers, Gypsy Rose Lee, and the Ramones have performed here. Now, the 1,000-seat venue books successful touring rock and hip-hop acts. ◈ Map J4 • 1426 1st Ave • (206) 628-0221

2 Dimitriou's Jazz Alley

A solid anchor in the Seattle music scene, Dimitriou's Jazz Alley has been bringing the best jazz, swing, and blues musicians to the Northwest since 1979. Among the big acts that have performed here are the Count Basie Orchestra, Eartha Kitt, Taj Mahal, and Dr. John. The venue is classy and intimate; be prepared for an outstanding evening. There are dinner shows, as well as music-only shows. ◈ Map J3 • 2033 6th Ave • (206) 441-9729

The Triple Door

3 Chop Suey

This club dominates the smoke-filled, hard rock scene on Capitol Hill, but does so with style and flair. Glowing red lights and lanterns shed a bit of light, while images of Bruce Lee add to the kitschy theme. Most of the acts are local or regional rock outfits, although hip-hop rules on Sunday nights. ◈ Map E4 • 1325 E Madison St • (206) 324-8005

4 Tractor Tavern

A bastion of great music, this place thrives as an alternative to clubs elsewhere in Seattle that are known for mining hard rock acts. The Tractor primarily books bands with repertoire in the vein of country and western, rockabilly, bluegrass, or musicians who seamlessly fuse all those styles into something quite original. ◈ Map B2 • 5213 Ballard Ave NW • (206) 789-3599

5 Nectar Lounge

This happening Fremont club has live music seven nights a week, ranging from indie to hip-hop, reggae to dance, folk, funk, punk, and more. They book a good range of national and local acts. There are three bars and an attractive outdoor patio with a fireplace, making this a favorite spot for younger Seattleites. Bar food and a good selection of pizzas are also available. ◈ Map D2 • 412 N 36th St • (206) 632-2020

Using the word "grunge" to describe Seattle's music will mark you as an unhip outsider or a journalist looking for verbal shortcuts.

Gallery 1412

Gallery 1412 is a collectively owned musical arts venue with an imposing artistic vision. The award-winning curators book acts dedicated to experimental music in a no-frills setting. Patrons listen and learn about contemporary composition, electroacoustic and electronic music, free improvization, and jazz. ◈ *Map E5 • 1412 18th Ave • (206) 322-1533*

The Triple Door

In the space of a former 1920s-era vaudeville theater upscale audiences soak up the best of jazz, rock, cabaret, and blues while enjoying French wine and cuisine. ◈ *Map J4 • 216 Union St • (206) 838-4333*

El Corazón

Formerly known as Graceland, El Corazón proudly flaunts its roots as a crusty, smoky rock club. It's a mecca for those seeking strong drinks and a favorite venue for many of the area's hard-working rock bands. ◈ *Map L3 • 109 Eastlake Ave E • (206) 262-0482*

Sunset Tavern

This tavern is primarily an outlet for start-up bands of the ear-shattering punk rock persuasion. The room's red decor and lighting seems to take inspiration from a Victorian bordello. Lots of bands have their first gigs here. ◈ *Map B1 • 5433 Ballard Ave NW • (206) 784-4880*

Neumo's

Once known as Moe's, this is Capitol Hill's most hip and happening music venue. The club is back to basics, with a strong show of rock bands and DJ dance nights. ◈ *Map M3 • 925 E Pike St • (206) 709-9467*

Top 10 Local Microbrews

1 Redhook
The area's earliest microbrewery began in May 1981. ◈ *Map P2 • 14300 NE 145th St, Woodinville*

2 Hale's Ales Brewery
Savor delicious brews and pub grub. ◈ *Map C2 • 4301 Leary Way NW • (206) 706-1544*

3 Maritime Pacific Brewing Company
Order a pint of Nightwatch at this tavern. ◈ *Map C2 • 1111 NW Ballard Way • (206) 782-6181*

4 Elliott Bay Brewing Company
West Seattle's bastion of microbrew and pub fare. ◈ *Map A6 • 4720 California Ave SW • (206) 932-8695*

5 McMenamins
Six Arms is a popular branch of the McMenamins chain. ◈ *Map E4 • 300 E Pike St • (206) 223-1648*

6 Elysian Brewing Company
The Hill's best pub makes legendary brews. ◈ *Map M3 • 1221 E Pike St • (206) 860-1920*

7 Pyramid Alehouse, Brewery & Restaurant
Excellent beers and faux-Egyptian labels. ◈ *Map D6 • 1201 1st Ave S • (206) 682-3377*

8 Big Time Brewery & Alehouse
Sample handcrafted ales. ◈ *Map E2 • 4133 University Way NE • (206) 545-4509*

9 Pike Brewing Company
Best for microbrew, pub food, or brewing supplies. ◈ *Map J4 • 1415 1st Ave • (206) 622-6044*

10 Mac & Jack's
Try the African Amber. ◈ *Map P2 • 17825 NE 65th St, Redmond • (425) 558-9697*

The drinking age for all alcoholic beverages in Washington is 21, so have your ID handy when seeking entrance to taverns or bars.

Left **Metropolitan Grill** Right **Dahlia Lounge**

🔟 Restaurants

1 The Herbfarm

Dining at this Eastside restaurant requires time, money, and an appreciation of the culinary arts. Chef Chris Weber's kitchen often uses ingredients from the restaurant's gardens and farm. Creative menus include a nine-course dinner of Northwest foods, served with five or six matched wines (non alcoholic options are also available). Reserve well in advance. ⊗ Map P2 • 14590 NE 145th St, Woodinville • (425) 485-5300 • $$$$$

2 Ray's Boathouse & Café

This Ballard waterfront restaurant has two dining rooms. The café caters to happy-hour revelers, families, and informal diners, while the boathouse is reservation-only seating. Both menus includes the freshest Dungeness crab, oysters, and wild salmon from Alaska.
⊗ Map A1 • 6049 Seaview Ave NW
• (206) 789-3770 • $$$ (café; $$$$$ (boathouse)

3 Ponti Seafood Grill

Ponti creates sumptuous Pacific Rim dinners and hearty weekend brunches inside a Mediterranean-style villa. The chef fuses Asian herbs and spices with ahi tuna, scallops, and crab providing a harmonious meeting place for green curries and *fruits de la mer*. ⊗ Map C2
• 3014 3rd Ave N • (206) 284-3000 • $$$$

Dungeness crab

4 Metropolitan Grill

One of Seattle's most loved and traditional steakhouses draws in a faithful cadre of politicians and corporate attorneys every day. Portions are typically huge – salads, appetizers, baked potatoes, everything – so bring lots of friends for sharing. ⊗ Map K5
• 820 2nd Ave • (206) 624-3287 • $$$$$

5 Canlis

Treat your eyes and palate to dinner at Canlis. Specialties include Alaska halibut, Dungeness crab, Wagyu-style tenderloin, and a comprehensive and expensive wine selection. For a memorable occasion at Canlis, reserve the private cache room for two, and order in advance to ensure a serving of the luscious chocolate lava cake. ⊗ Map D3 • 2576 Aurora Ave N • (206) 283-3313 • $$$$$

6 Lark

Located in a converted 1917 warehouse with 25-ft- (7.6-m-) high ceilings, chef John Sundstrom's Lark is one of the Pacific Northwest's most lauded restaurants. Known for working with local farmers to provide seasonal dishes, the inviting menu features delicious, fresh small plates of locally produced cheese, vegetables, charcuterie, fish, and meat (see p77). ⊗ Map M4
• 952 E Seneca St • (206) 323-5275
• www.larkseattle.com • $$

For a guide to restaurant price ranges **See p67**

The Herbfarm

The Brooklyn Seafood, Steak & Oyster House

The not-to-be-missed dish here is the fresh local oysters. Classic cocktails at great prices during happy hour, and consistently excellent service, complete the experience at this centrally located, popular spot. Ⓢ Map K4 • 1212 2nd Ave • (206) 395-9227 • www.thebrooklyn.com • $$$

The Walrus and the Carpenter

Try the steak tartare and the freshly caught oysters at this crowded, trendy seafood restaurant. Expect to line up on weekends (they don't take reservations). Ⓢ Map C2 • 4743 Ballard Ave NW • (206) 395-9227 • $$$$

Café Juanita

This decorated Kirkland restaurant is renowned for its passion for Northern Italian food and wine. The lengthy menu reflects the kitchen's commitment to organic, sustainable ingredients. Exceptional service and a calm, classy dining room round out the experience. Ⓢ Map P2 • 9702 NE 120th Place, Kirkland • (425) 823-1505 • www.cafejuanita.com • $$$$$

Dahlia Lounge

Owner-chef Tom Douglas was one of the area's first fusion chefs, blending flavors into cohesive and tasty concoctions. Traditional dinner items such as crab cakes are favorites. Next door is the sweet tooth's haven, Dahlia Bakery. Ⓢ Map J3 • 2001 4th Ave • (206) 682-4142 • $$$$

Top 10 Sushi Restaurants

1 Musashi's
This minuscule joint buzzes with customers, as servings are generous and prices are astonishingly low. Ⓢ Map D2 • 1400 N 45th St • (206) 633-0212

2 Shiki Japanese Restaurant
A casual spot for authentic sashimi and sushi. Ⓢ Map G1 • 4 W Roy St • (206) 281-1352

3 Kozue
This place has its own loyal following. Ⓢ Map D2 • 1608 N 45th St • (206) 547-2008

4 Hana
Step in for the tastiest and least costly raw fish. Ⓢ Map M2 • 219 Broadway E • (206) 328-1187

5 Maneki
Try to reserve a private tatami room if you have a large group. Ⓢ Map L6 • 304 6th Ave S • (206) 622-2631

6 Shiro's
Watch as master chef Shiro Kashiba prepares your succulent sushi. Ⓢ Map H3 • 2401 2nd Ave • (206) 443-9844

7 Wasabi Bistro
Their tempura rolls are lavish and unique. Ⓢ Map J3 • 2311 2nd Ave • (206) 441-6044

8 Chiso
Serves imaginatively prepared sushi and sashimi. Ⓢ Map D2 • 3520 Fremont Ave N • (206) 632-3430

9 Azuma
Chef-owner prepares a small selection of fresh fish. Ⓢ Map A6 • 4533 California Ave SW • (206) 937-1148

10 I Love Sushi
This waterfront hideaway attracts crowds, as fish is always fresh. Ⓢ Map K1 • 1001 Fairview Ave N • (206) 625-9604

Left **Westlake Center exterior** Right **Westlake Center interior**

Stores & Shopping Centers

Pacific Place
Part of a $500-million development plan, Pacific Place is the crown jewel of Seattle's retail shopping centers. Stores include Tiffany & Co., Coach, Ann Taylor, Guess, Lulumon, L'Occitane, Aveda, and Williams-Sonoma. The top level has an 11-screen AMC Theatre complex and several fine gourmet restaurants. To top it off, there is also a skybridge connection to Nordstrom's flagship store. ◉ *Map K4 • 600 Pine St • (206) 405-2655*

5th Avenue Boutiques
A collection of boutiques between Union and Spring Streets caters to customers for whom price is no object. Fox's Gem Shop, Brooks Brothers, and St. John Boutique are the best stops for fine gems and jewelry and high fashion galore. ◉ *Map K4*

Pacific Place shopping center

University Village
Renovated and repositioned as a stellar shopping destination, this open-air mall just east of the UW has lovely landscaped walkways, fountains, restaurants, and stores that no longer attract just the resident graduate student population. Key stores include the Apple Store, Sony, The North Face, Gap, Ann Taylor Restoration Hardware, and Banana Republic. ◉ *Map F2 • 4500 25th Ave NE • (206) 523-0622*

Westlake Center
The center has a four-tiered glass-enclosed atrium stacked with small regionally based shops, several chain stores, and a large food court. Made in Washington, Lush, Fireworks, Mix, Jessica McClintock, and Nature's are well worth visiting. Outside, Westlake Plaza attracts workers on break and also features seasonal concerts and public events. ◉ *Map K4 • 400 Pine St • (206) 467-1600*

Nordstrom
John W. Nordstrom's *(see p31)* shoe store, opened with his Alaska Gold Rush earnings in 1901, is now synonymous with impeccable service and quality merchandise. Hunting for fine apparel, elegant shoes, exquisite handbags, or other accessories can be exhausting, so step into the in-store spa and salon for a pampering experience. ◉ *Map K4 • 500 Pine St • (206) 628-2111*

Rainier Tower

Macy's

For less extravagant spenders, there's what used to be the locally owned Bon Marche. The new name reflects investment and ownership by the famous Chicago department store chain, but locals still refer to this large store simply as the Bon. Find everything from linen to lingerie, and loveseats to luggage, all at reasonable prices. ✪ *Map J4 • 1601 3rd Ave • (206) 506-6000*

North of the Market to Belltown

A stroll along First and Second Avenues in the Belltown area leads to this ultrahip shopping destination. There are boutique shoe stores, upscale bathroom fixtures and furnishing stores, art galleries, wine cellars, and many other intriguing stores to beckon in curious shoppers. And, when you need a rest, there is no shortage of restaurants, coffee shops, or bars, either. ✪ *Map J4*

Wallingford Center

For a real taste of Seattle's charming Wallingford neighborhood, discover a variety of local commerce along 45th Street, such as restaurants and shops, as well as the Wallingford Center, a converted turn-of-the-19th-century elementary school.

Quite a few of these shops are for or about children, including L'il Klippers (haircuts). ✪ *Map D2 • 1815 N 45th St • (206) 517-7773*

Rainier Square

A cavernous mini-city of upscale shops selling everything from imported chocolate to Louis Vuitton designer goods is in the base of Rainier Tower (see p33). Find entrances on any of the four sides of the complex, which occupies an entire city block. Be sure to visit the Jeffrey Moose Gallery for the latest in painting and sculpture. The underground concourse links up with the Washington State Convention Center (see p63). ✪ *Map K4 • 1310 5th Ave*

Westfield Southcenter

With over 200 shops and services, this is the largest shopping center in the Pacific Northwest. Key stores include JCPenney, Macy's, Nordstrom's, Sears, J.Crew, Abercrombie & Fitch, Pandora, Bebe, and Sephora. There are also plenty of restaurants, a food court facing Mount Rainier, a 16-screen AMC movie theater, and a rainforest-themed play area for kids. Located in the suburban city of Tukwila. ✪ *Map P3 • 2800 Southcenter Mall • (206) 246-0423*

Left **Floating bridges** Right **Skyline of Bellevue**

🔟 The Eastside

1 Floating Bridges

Lake Washington's famous floating bridges, Interstate 90 and State Route 520, connect Seattle with Bellevue and the Eastside. Both highways resemble ordinary bridges except for the middle portions, which rest on the water's surface above air-filled pontoons that support tons of traffic and concrete. Occasional windstorms push waves of water onto the road, creating back-ups for commuters. ✎ *Map P2*

2 Kirkland

Once a small rural town across Lake Washington, Kirkland has grown into a sprawling suburb with resident Microsoft executives and managers giving it a reputation for expensive real estate. It's also known for a charming waterfront that offers great shopping and dining and fantastic beaches that provide views of Seattle and the Olympic Mountains. ✎ *Map P2*

3 Old Bellevue

Bellevue sometimes gets a bad rap from more city-slicked Seattleites. It's a classic suburb, as well as one of the state's largest cities. But there is an area that speaks of its former life as a small town. Head to Old Bellevue and its restored Main Street for the antidote to freeway interchanges and big box stores, especially if you like buying antiques. ✎ *Map P2*

4 Eastside Wineries

Tip your glass of red wine during a visit to Chateau Ste. Michelle, Washington state's oldest winery. Their 87-acre (35-ha) wooded estate in Woodinville, 15 miles (24 km) north of Seattle, hosts tours and well-attended summer concerts. It's one of several outfits taking advantage of a climate that favors excellent grape varieties. Other producers of good-quality wine include Columbia Crest, DeLille Cellars, and family-owned and operated Facelli Winery. ✎ *Chateau Ste. Michelle: Map P2 • 14111 NE 145th St, Woodinville*

5 The Gates Estate

So many people wonder how and where one of the world's richest men lives. Microsoft's founder, Bill Gates, built his estate on Lake Washington's eastern shore installing the latest technological advancements in modern living – high-end security systems, customized touch and voice controls, and luxurious

A wine cellar

Marymoor Park

entertainment facilities. The estate is not open to the public, naturally, but it's visible from the water and touring boats occasionally cruise within sight from a considerable distance. ✪ *Map P2 • 1835 73rd Ave NE, Medina*

Crossroads Shopping Center

This bustling shopping center is popular with Microsoft employees and vibrant ethnic groups, sometimes in traditional regalia. Free jazz, folk, and world music concerts on a professional stage and public art installations help make this a gathering place with personality. ✪ *Map P2 • 15600 NE 8th St, Bellevue • (425) 644-1111*

Mercer Slough Nature Park

This 320-acre (129-ha) park on the grounds of the largest remaining wetland on Lake Washington has a 7-mile (11-km) network of trails and esplanades. Bird-watchers flock to the Slough to view 100 species; other wildlife includes coyote, beaver, and muskrat. Activities comprise canoeing and kayaking, guided nature walks, and u-pick blueberries during the summer season. ✪ *Map P2 • 2102 Bellevue Way SE, Bellevue*

Marymoor Park

The county's most popular park, located in Redmond, maintains soccer and baseball fields, a velodrome, and an off-leash dog-training field. Dogs are free to roam and splash in water, a practice seriously discouraged or outlawed everywhere else. Park trails connect with the Sammamish River Trail, a bike route that leads to popular wineries in Woodinville. ✪ *Map P2 • 6046 W Lake Sammamish Pkwy NE, Redmond*

Luther Burbank Park

Mercer Island is a small affluent community off Interstate 90 near Lake Washington's eastern shore. The lovely waterfront park, on the northeastern tip of the island, offers boaters and visitors notable attractions such as tennis courts, a playground, and trails that lead to a swimming area and fishing dock. On summer Sunday afternoons, the park hosts free concerts in its amphitheater. ✪ *Map P2 • 2040 84th Ave SE, Mercer Island*

Microsoft Visitor Center

Learn more about the history, products, and vision of the software giant at this high-tech visitor center located on their Redmond campus. Big screens, interactive exhibits, and a 30-year timeline bring the culture of Microsoft to life. You can check out the latest developments in gaming, mobile devices, and much more. ✪ *Map P2 • 15010 NE 36th St, Redmond • (425) 703-6214*

Left **San Juan Island** Center **Lighthouse, Pt. Townsend** Right **Ann Starrett Mansion, Pt. Townsend**

Day Trips: Islands & Historic Towns

1 Bainbridge Island

The ferry ride to Winslow on Bainbridge Island (from downtown Seattle's Pier 52) should be mandatory for tourists who want an inspiring view of the Seattle skyline. A stroll from the terminal to Winslow's quaint waterfront shops and cafés has its own rewards. ® *Map N2*

2 Vashon Island

Vashon's gentle, two-lane roads make it a favorite destination for both bicyclists and motorcyclists looking for a quick and unique getaway to the countryside. Board the Fauntleroy Ferry *(see p97)* in West Seattle to discover the island's huge estates, arts and crafts galleries, berry and alpaca farms, and a subculture of 1960s-style progressives. ® *Map N3*

3 Whidbey Island

As the longest island in the western contiguous United States, Whidbey Island's ample waterfront real estate makes it vacation-home-central. The island's six state parks, historic forts, and tiny seaside villages attract weekend crowds. It is also the perfect location for the area's largest US Navy air base. Their sign reads, "Pardon our noise, it's the sound of freedom". ® *Map P1*

4 San Juan Islands

In the far northwest of Washington state lies the San Juan archipelago, comprising 700 islands, of which only 177 have names. Ferries sail from Anacortes to the four largest islands – Lopez, Shaw, San Juan, and Orcas. Lopez is great for cycling. Hilly Orcas offers breathtaking views from atop Mt. Constitution. At 2,409 ft (734 m), it provides the best viewpoint of the area's stunning geographical features. San Juan, with the largest town (Friday Harbor), is best for walk-on passengers. Be sure to check out the Whale Museum if you visit. Shaw Island does not offer visitor facilities. ® *Map N4*

5 Tacoma

Founded as a sawmill town in the 1860s, Tacoma is known for its historic buildings and strong architectural symbols, which includes the 1893 Italianate tower of Old City Hall. The impressive Chihuly Bridge of Glass links the Museum of Glass to downtown Tacoma and the imaginative Washington State History Museum. Explore the small but impressive Tacoma Art Museum, and Point Defiance Zoo and Aquarium, highlighting a Pacific Rim theme. ® *Map P3*

Tacoma Museum of Glass

 If you need a ferry and prefer not to miss the boat, avoid rush hours and arrive at least 45 minutes before ferry departure.

Leavenworth

In an effort to revive the dying logging town, civic leaders came up with the German theme in the 1970s. The town, with its Bavarian-styled architecture, now bustles with festivals, art shows, and summer theater productions. Another popular attraction is the Leavenworth Nutcracker Museum. Ⓢ Map Q5

Horse-drawn beer wagon, Leavenworth

Olympia

Washington's state capital has a rich past, historic buildings, and a thriving youth culture. Highlights include the State Capitol Campus, with grounds designed by the Olmsted Brothers in 1928, Evergreen State College, a farmers' market, and the surrounding mostly rural Thurston County.
Ⓢ Map P5

Roslyn

The model for Cicely, Alaska, in the television show *Northern Exposure*, Roslyn has its own history unrelated to the quirky profiles offered in Hollywood's depiction. In this mining boomtown, late 19th-century coal companies imported workers of various nationalities, as is evident from the tombs in the cemetery, grouped as they are in 26 'segregated' areas. Roslyn is on the National Historic Register. Ⓢ Map Q6

Port Townsend

This idyllic seaport, on the northeast tip of the Olympic Peninsula, attracts artists and musicians. Known for its Victorian architecture, key sights include Jefferson County Historical Society, Ann Starrett Mansion, Fire Bell Tower, and Fort Worden State Park. The small town has a bustling waterfront with shops, cafés, restaurants, and a ferry terminal. Ⓢ Map N1

Victoria, BC

Catch a ferry or seaplane to British Columbia's provincial capital, Victoria. Established as a Hudson's Bay Company fur-trading post in 1843, it has become a favorite destination for Anglophiles who queue up at the grand Fairmont Empress Hotel for traditional tea and cakes. Other attractions include the Inner Harbor, the Royal British Columbia Museum, and Butchart Gardens – an amazing collection of flora planted in a sprawling former quarry. Ⓢ Map N4

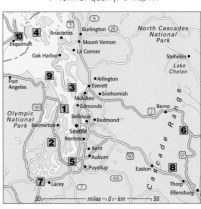

For more information on ferry departures, call (206) 464-6400 or log onto www.wsdot.wa.gov/ferries

Hikers at Paradise, Mount Rainier

Day Trips: Mountain Getaways

Mount Rainier
This silent, snowcapped sentinel, the centerpiece of Mount Rainier National Park, is an awe-inspiring active volcano rising 14,410-ft (4,392-m) above sea level. The Grand Dame of the Cascades commands great respect for its potentially devastating force; it has more glacial ice – and populated surrounds – than St Helens. ◈ Map P6

View of Mount Rainier

Mount Si
Seattle's closest Cascade Mountain, the rocky outcropping of Mount Si is just past Issaquah. The hike is steep but not too difficult, and the views of the Snoqualmie Valley watershed and I-90 are rewarding. ◈ Map Q5

Issaquah Alps
This series of foothills west of the Cascades are remnants of mountains that predate the higher and more visited peaks to the east. Cougar, Squak, Tiger, and Rattlesnake Mountains are four main park areas that attract individuals and families seeking woodland walks without steep drops or high altitude. ◈ Map P3

Snoqualmie Falls
Local Native American tribes regarded Snoqualmie Falls as a sacred place. The 268-ft (82-m) waterfall, beautifully divided in two sections by a convenient rock outcropping, marks the end of the Cascade Plateau, where the Snoqualmie River begins its final descent to the sea. An observation deck and a steep path to the river allow for close-up breathtaking views. ◈ Map Q3

Twin Falls
Hikers wanting a short spell of deep woods and water head to Olallie State Park, where a 3-mile (5-km) trail to Twin Falls awaits. The park's amazing plant life includes giant ferns and salmonberry, and some of the Cascades' few old-growth trees. One Douglas fir has a circumference of 14 ft (4 m). ◈ Map Q5

Denny Creek
Hiking near Snoqualmie Pass along I-90 is a mecca for families with kids. The creek pours over a series of rocks and creates pools for perfect old-fashioned swimming hole fun. ◈ Map Q5

Tonga Ridge
The 6.5-mile (10-km) trail in the Alpine Lakes Wilderness offers a pleasant walk through forests and wild berry picking when the season's right. Meadows bloom in a kaleidoscope of colors in late spring, and mountain scenery abounds. ◈ Map Q5

Carry proper supplies for hiking in the mountains. **See p45**

Snoqualmie Falls

Staircase Rapids
The ferry crossing and subsequent scenic drive along the Hood Canal enhance the journey to these rapids. The popular route inches near the fast-flowing Skokomish River as it pours down the eastern slopes of the Olympic Range on its way to Lake Cushman. Look out for kingfishers, harlequin ducks, and giant salamanders on the 2-mile (3-km) loop. ◎ Map N5

Hurricane Ridge
Drive to this 5,230-ft (1,594-m) mountain top at one of Olympic National Park's most visited sites. The routes are paved, and bring visitors to one of the best 360-degree alpine overlooks. In winter, when the snowpack is immensely deep, the roads remain open for skiers and snowshoers. ◎ Map N5

Big Four Ice Caves
Global warming has taken a toll on ice caves, but the attraction at the base of 6,153-ft (1,875-m) Big Four Mountain in the North Cascades is still vital. Hike the 1-mile (1.6-km) trail off the Mountain Loop Highway to the Ice Caves, the unusual result of alpine avalanches and climate conditions impacting the ice field at the mountain's base. ◎ Map P5

Top 10 Features of Mount Rainier

1 Paradise
Leads to wildflower-filled meadows, and trails starting at 5,400-ft (1,646-m) to moraines and majestic views of the Nisqually Glacier.

2 Sunrise
Recommended as starting point for solitary hikes.

3 Summit Climb
A round-trip to the crater and back requires training, professional gear, and a few days. Hire a guide or go with a group if you're not a seasoned climber.

4 Family Day Hikes
Dozens of trails for family day trips and picnics are available; try one out near the Carbon River entrance.

5 Wonderland Trail
This 93-mile (149-km) trail through several mini-ecosystems around the mountain is ideal for serious backpackers with weeks to spare.

6 Cloud Lid
Rainier's cloud cover often resembles a flying saucer hovering above the peak.

7 Glacial Melting
Climate changes have decreased the area of Rainier's permanent snow cap and facilitated glacial retreats.

8 Jökulhlaups & Lahars
Glacial floods and debris flows can move at speeds up to 60 mph (95.5 km/h).

9 Sleeping Giant
Experts agree that it's a question of when, and not if, Mount Rainier's active volcano will blow again.

10 Pollution's Effects
Smog from automobile traffic now obscures the mountain more and more.

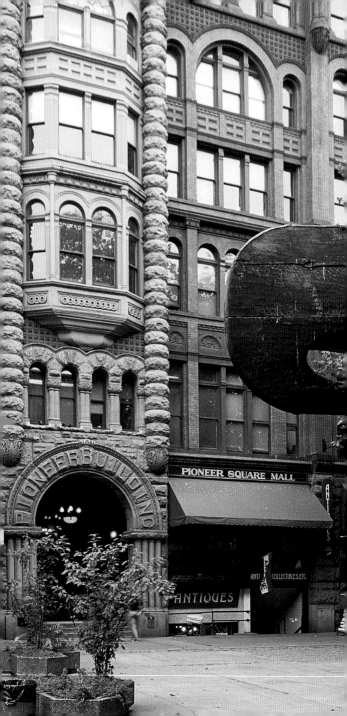

AROUND
TOWN

Downtown
62–69

Capitol Hill
70–77

Fremont
80–87

Ballard
88–93

West Seattle
96–101

SEATTLE'S TOP 10

Left **Pike Place Market** Center **Totem poles, Pioneer Square** Right **Seattle Great Wheel**

Downtown

W HAT STRIKES MANY VISITORS to downtown Seattle is how easy it is to see the sights, since many key attractions lie within walking distance of one another. Bookended by Belltown to the north and Pioneer Square to the south, the downtown area can be explored on foot or with the help of the city's buses. The waterfront also boasts many attractions as well as superb views. In addition to being a business district full of skyscrapers, downtown offers a wide range of options – such as gourmet restaurants, attractive shopping centers and upscale boutiques, and a perfect place from which to begin exploring the city.

Left **Rachel the pig, Pike Place Market** Right **Pike Place Market stalls**

🔟 Sights

1. Pike Place Market
2. Seattle Art Museum
3. Harbor Steps
4. Washington State Convention Center/ Freeway Park
5. Columbia Center
6. Pioneer Square
7. Central Library
8. Seattle Center Monorail
9. Belltown
10. Seattle Great Wheel

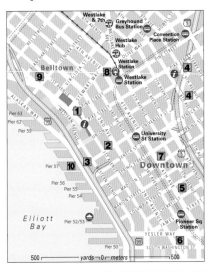

Previous pages **Totem pole at Pioneer Square**

Harbor Steps

If you happen to be near the Seattle Art Museum on First Avenue and need to get down to the waterfront, try the Harbor Steps. A street's abrupt end has been turned into a wide-open stairway landscaped with water sculpture and planters. The steps are spacious and an ideal urban meeting place, located below a *nouveau* luxury apartment complex in the heart of an ever-changing downtown Seattle. Countless restaurant and nightlife options abound in the vicinity. ◈ *Map J5*

Fish-flinging fishmongers

Pike Place Market

Anyone descending on Pike Place Market to stroll by innumerable stalls of seafood, fresh produce, crafts, and flower bouquets can feel the rapid pulse of a scene that's all about hard work and hustle. The market is famous for its salmon-throwing fishmongers and street musicians who entertain tourists daily. *See pp8–9.*

Seattle Art Museum

Designed by Venturi Scott Brown and Associates, the imposing sandstone and limestone edifice is now connected seamlessly to the spacious and light-filled 2007 expansion, designed by Brad Cloepfil of Allied Works Architecture. SAM now accommodates major touring exhibitions as well as an impressive permanent collection of over 23,000 works of ancient to modern art, including Native American, Asian, African, Australian Aboriginal, European, and Islamic art. The museum's Olympic Sculpture Park *(see p13)* at the north end of downtown showcases unique sculptures in a stunning waterfront setting. *See p36.*

Washington State Convention Center/ Freeway Park

Straddling Interstate 5 in a miraculous feat of engineering, the Washington State Convention Center is located within easy walking distance of the city's best shops, hotels, and restaurants. Marvel at the center's 90-ft- (27-m-) wide glass canopy bridge that frames views to Elliott Bay and to the historic Pike-Pine neighborhood. Adjoining is Freeway Park, where blossoms delight visitors in spring and waterfalls mask the sounds of traffic flowing on all sides. ◈ *Washington State Convention Center: Map K4; 800 Convention Place; (206) 694-5000; www.wscc.com*
• *Freeway Park: Map K4*

Washington State Convention Center

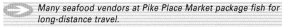

Many seafood vendors at Pike Place Market package fish for long-distance travel.

The awe-inspiring Columbia Center

Columbia Center

The sleek, three-tiered black skyscraper that dominates Seattle's skyline might have been even taller, but for an order to reduce the ultimate height from the Federal Aviation Administration. To break a record for most floors in any one building, the builder kept the original 76 stories but reduced the ceiling heights to compensate. The 1985 building has an observation deck on the 73rd floor that offers panoramic views of Elliott Bay and Mount Rainier. *See p32.*

Pioneer Square

Find art galleries, intricate Victorian architecture, bookstores, and cafés in a constantly changing National Historic District. Pioneer Square's 20-block neighborhood became Seattle's commercial center during the boom years of logging, fishing, railroads, and Klondike Gold Rush economies. An exclusive 90-minute underground tour *(see p14)* offers a lively look at the 19th-century storefronts that were periodically flooded by tides from Elliott Bay until street

levels were raised. A key sight is the Smith Tower, and art lovers will enjoy an art walk that takes place on the first Thursday night of each month. *Map K5*

Central Library

The downtown library is, in itself, a work of art. Nearly 8,000 patrons per day benefit from more than 1.45 million books and reference materials, Internet access, spacious areas for children, and over 400 public computers. The art collection alone is valued at $1 million. *See p32.*

Seattle Center Monorail

For an adventurous and fun way to travel the 1 mile (1.6 km) between downtown's Westlake Center and the Seattle Center, hop aboard the Monorail and experience the future of mass transit from the perspective of engineers who built the elevated rail as an attraction for the 1962 World's Fair. The first commercial monorail in the United States, it continues to use the original cars, and makes the 2-minute journey every 10 minutes. *See pp11 & 32.*

Denny Regrade

Named after one of the city's founders, Arthur A. Denny, Denny Hill would have certainly become one of Seattle's most upscale neighborhoods, with magnificent city, mountain, and water views. However, in 1905, engineers began its outright removal by extracting the mud with water jets and conveyor belts, eventually dumping the debris into Elliott Bay. Today, the unnaturally flat, 50-square-block area includes most of what's now called Belltown, and is occupied largely by condos, restaurants, and social agencies.

Head inside Central Library for a visual treat that is as spectacular as the glass and steel exterior shell.

Monorail at Seattle Center Station

Belltown

Pedestrians are welcomed with an explosion of shops, clubs, cafés, luxury condos, and fine restaurants. This upscale neighborhood was named in the 1970s after a pioneer, William M. Bell. In those days, Belltown attracted sailors on shore leave, artists seeking inexpensive loft spaces, and ragtag urban dwellers. But it was the dot.com boom of the 1990s that changed everything by engendering a commercial revival for the neighborhood. Remnants of old Belltown include a few well-preserved facades. Map J4

Seattle Great Wheel

At the end of Pier 57, on the Seattle waterfront, the wheel *(see p12)* sits 175 ft (53 m) above the pier and extends nearly 40 ft (12 m) over Elliott Bay. The views are spectacular from each of the 42 climate-controlled, fully enclosed gondolas. One rotation takes around 20 minutes and, for an extra cost, a VIP gondola is available, with leather seating and a glass bottom. Map J5 • (206) 623-8600 • Summer: 10am–11pm Sun–Thu, 10am–midnight Fri–Sat (winter hours may vary) • Adm: $13 adults, $8.50 children (4–11) • www.seattlegreatwheel.com

Downtown Shopping Spree

Mid-morning

Stop at **Westlake Center** *(see p52)* and grab an espresso and pastry at the stand in the plaza before window-shopping Westlake's indoor mall. Inside, **Made in Washington** offers a large and creative inventory of regionally produced merchandise. Walk across Pine Street to find **Nordstrom's** spacious flagship store *(see p52)*, stocked with top designer brands and the absolute best of everything. Splurge in **Pacific Place** mall *(see p52)*, where you can choose from upmarket stores including Tiffany & Co., Coach, Ann Taylor, and Williams-Sonoma. Exit the mall on Pine, turn right, and then left on 5th Avenue to University Street for pricey boutiques and fine jewelry, such as **Fox's Gem Shop** (1341 5th Ave).

Descend into the cavernous indoor mall at **Rainier Square** *(see p53)*, underneath the white high-rise that rests on a narrow pedestal. The base of the building opens up for a city block's worth of shops, galleries, and restaurants. Look for fine art in the **Jeffrey Moose Gallery** and luxury bed linen from **Duxiana**. Walk downhill on University to 4th Avenue, where you can board a number of non-express buses for a ride back to Pike Street, or stay on the bus a few more blocks to Virginia Street for a superb Italian lunch at **Assaggio** *(see p67)*. Ask the driver for help if you need it.

Left **Moore Theatre** Center **The Art Institute of Seattle** Right **Austin A. Bell Building**

🔟 Around Belltown

1 Lenora Street Bridge
This elegant footbridge leads from Western Avenue to the Elliott Bay piers, providing stellar views of West Seattle and the Olympic Mountains. 🖎 *Map H4*

2 Whiskey Bar
This trendy bar in Belltown offers a large variety of whiskey. Good for pre-concert gatherings due to its proximity to the Moore Theatre. 🖎 *Map J4 • 2000 2nd Ave*

3 Belltown Billiards
A mix of professional-quality billiard tables with sumptuous Italian fare, DJs, and live music creates a hopping late-night scene. 🖎 *Map H4 • 90 Blanchard St*

4 Rendezvous
This bar houses the minuscule Jewel Box Theater, a 1926-era private movie-screening room, while the remodeled bar draws hipsters and condo-dwellers. 🖎 *Map H3 • 2322 2nd Ave*

5 Top Pot Doughnuts
Take a hiatus from healthful dining and grab a few doughnuts from this stylish café that welcomes loungers sipping coffee and dipping tasty treats. 🖎 *Map J3 • 2124 5th Ave*

6 Sub Pop World Headquarters
The local record label created by Jonathan Poneman and Bruce Pavitt in the mid-1980s signed bands such as Nirvana and Soundgarden that put Seattle on the rock music map worldwide. 🖎 *Map H3 • 2013 4th Ave*

7 Waterfront Station
Stations near Piers 66, 67, and 69 are all you will see of the Waterfront Trolley, since the trolley barn was demolished to make way for the Olympic Sculpture Park. A replacement bus (No. 99) runs between the ID, Pioneer Square, and the Waterfront. 🖎 *Map H4*

8 Austin A. Bell Building
Elmer Fisher, Seattle's foremost commercial architect, designed this handsome building that reflects Richardsonian, Gothic, and Italianate styles. It houses pricey condos and a nightclub. 🖎 *Map H3 • 2326 1st Ave*

9 The Art Institute of Seattle
The institute offers programs in the areas of design, fashion, media and culinary arts. 🖎 *Map H4 • 2323 Elliott Ave • (206) 448-6600*

🔟 Moore Theatre
This historic theater stages theatrical productions, concerts, and lectures. 🖎 *Map J4 • 1932 2nd Ave*

66

Price Categories

Price categories include a three-course meal for one, two glasses of wine and all unavoidable extra charges including tax.	
$	under $20
$$	$20–$40
$$$	$40–$55
$$$$	$55–$80
$$$$$	over $80

Dahlia Lounge

Belltown Places to Eat

1 Local 360
Earnest, community-minded restaurant that sources ingredients from local farmers within a 360-mile (579-km) radius. Expect a casual, eclectic crowd. ◊ Map H3 • 2234 1st Ave • (206) 441-9360 • $$

2 Cyclops
Local customers return for their classic hummus plate, and both *Interview* and *Details* magazines have raved about the scene. Don't miss the roast chicken quesadilla. ◊ Map H3 • 2421 1st Ave • (206) 441-1677 • $$

3 Assaggio Ristorante
Savor tasty authentic Italian cuisine such as spaghetti carbonara, *pappardelle cinghiale* (wild boar sauce), and osso buco. Many of the desserts are imported from Italy and include favorites such as tiramisu. ◊ Map J3 • 2010 4th Ave • (206) 441-1399 • $$$

4 Dahlia Lounge
(See p51).

5 Queen City Grill
Treat yourself to a softly lit dining room, superb cocktails, great dishes such as grilled fish or lamb chops, and live jazz. ◊ Map J4 • 2201 1st Ave • (206) 443-0975 • $$$$

6 Two Bells Tavern
Great pub grub, especially burgers, and microbrews on tap. Occasional live music. ◊ Map J3 • 2313 4th Ave • (206) 441-3050 • $

7 Mama's Mexican Kitchen
Huge portions of Mexican classics (burritos, tacos, enchiladas) and strong margaritas served up in a weird and wacky environment. ◊ Map J3 • 2234 2nd Ave • (206) 728-6262 • $$

8 Belltown Pizza
With the atmosphere of a neighborhood bar, this pizzeria offers both standard and gourmet pizzas, which can be ordered by the slice. There is a small pasta selection; try the gorgonzola-and-walnut-stuffed ravioli. ◊ Map H3 • 2422 1st Ave • (206) 441-2653 • $$

9 Macrina Bakery
A cherished bakery café famous for bread pudding with fresh cream and berries, soups, salads, and sandwiches. ◊ Map H3 • 2408 1st Ave • (206) 448-4032 • $

10 El Gaucho
One of the city's premier steakhouses, where diners flock to order from an extensive menu featuring 28-day, dry-aged Angus prime beef, fresh seafood, and delicious side orders. ◊ Map H3 • 2505 1st Ave • (206) 728-1337 • $$$$

Left **Patagonia** Right **Paperhaus**

Belltown Shops

Baby & Co.
The place for European-styled slacks, skirts, dresses, and accessories for women. Look for designs by Maria Calderara, Hannes Roether, Frank & Eileen, and Marithé and François Girbaud. ◉ *Map J4 • 1936 1st Ave*

Paperhaus
Shop for contemporary presentation supplies and storage materials from award-winning manufacturers such as NAVA, Prat, and Rexite. Unique stationery, binders, or photo albums are also available.
◉ *Map J4 • 2008 1st Ave*

Vain
An innovative one-stop shop for hip consumers who need to mainline trendiness. Discover a full service salon, beauty supply store, independent designer boutique, and an artist gallery.
◉ *Map J4 • 2018 1st Ave*

Patagonia
Its roots as purveyor of first-rate gear, rugged wear, and polar fleece comfort began with alpinist and founder Yvon Chouinard. ◉ *Map J4 • 2100 1st Ave*

Robbins Brothers, The Engagement Ring Store
It would be hard to miss the arty neon sign of a bejeweled ring glowing above this tempting shop in Belltown. The staff is informed and easy-going.
◉ *Map J4 • 2200 1st Ave*

Karan Dannenberg Clothier
Offers original and elegant wear for the sophisticated shopper, but expect the silk suits and lace-trimmed casual items to be expensive. ◉ *Map J4 • 2232 1st Ave*

Endless Knot
Stocking sizes small to 3X, this popular shop marries elegance with the unusual. Artful designs with a contemporary Asian feel. ◉ *Map H3 • 2300 1st Ave*

Roq La Rue Gallery
Lowbrow art gallery that also sells interesting art books and prints. Friday night openings often feature live music and local and international artists. ◉ *Map H3 • 2312 2nd Ave • (206) 374-8977*

Esquin Wine Merchants
The city's oldest and largest wine retailer, Esquin has a cellar of around 4,000 different wines at any one time, and a large staff of experts is on hand to help you make your choice. Regular wine tastings are offered. ◉ *Map D6 • 2700 4th Ave S • Wine tastings: 5–6:30pm Thu, 2–7pm Sat*

Sell Your Sole Consignment Boutique
Friendly service and good-value prices can be found at this vintage women's clothing and shoes boutique. Designer labels include Alexander McQueen, Prada and Chanel. ◉ *Map J4 • 2121 1st Ave • (206) 443-2616*

 Save space in your luggage by asking stores to ship your purchases to your home or office.

Left **AllSaints** Center **Nancy Meyer** Right **Peter Miller**

TOP 10 Downtown Shops

Pendleton
Thomas Kay founded this popular retail outlet specializing in blankets and clothes for men and women. ✆ *Map K4 • 1313 4th Ave • www.pendleton-usa.com*

Bella Umbrella
To combat Seattle's notoriously rainy weather, invest in one of the top-notch umbrellas rented and sold at this friendly store. All shapes, sizes, and colors imaginable are available, from fashion and golf umbrellas to high-tech models and sun parasols. ✆ *Map J4 • 1535 1st Ave • www.bellaumbrella.com*

Mariners Team Store
Here's where to purchase official team jerseys and T-shirts, baseball caps, and other gift items emblazoned with the Seattle's winning professional league team logo. ✆ *Map J4 • 1800 4th Ave*

AllSaints
Trendy British clothing brand for women and men. Urban and cutting-edge designs are echoed in the warehouse-style store. ✆ *Map K4 • 1511 5th Ave & Pine • www.us.allsaints.com*

Metsker Maps of Seattle
Geography enthusiasts lose themselves in this impressive shop, where customers can peruse a variety of maps, travel guides, moon charts, and globes. ✆ *Map J4 • 1511 1st Ave • (206) 623-8747 • www.metskers.com*

Eddie Bauer
This store offers seasonal collections of all-occasion apparel, footwear, travel gear, and accessories for men and women. Founded in 1920 in Seattle, today more than 400 stores exist worldwide. ✆ *Map K4 • 600 Pine St • www.eddiebauer.com*

Nancy Meyer
Supplement your purchases of trendy outerwear with lingerie that's as sexy as it is elegant and tasteful. ✆ *Map K4 • 1318 5th Ave • www.nancymeyer.com*

Isadoras Antique Jewelry
New, designer, vintage, and private label, Isadora's collection of estate jewelry has been a hit since the late 1970s. Lots of incredible finds. ✆ *Map J4 • 1601 1st Ave • www.isadoras.com*

Peter Miller
A specialty bookstore that makes you feel sleek and creative. Scout for anything on architecture, graphic design, landscaping, and art in general, or Corbu letter stencils, planners, and art-imbibed gift items. ✆ *Map J4 • 1930 1st Ave • www.petermiller.com*

John Fluevog Shoes
High style and comfort are combined in John Fluevog's quirky designs. Prices are surprisingly affordable, and twice-yearly sales in January and July offer excellent value. ✆ *Map K4 • 205 Pine St • www.fluevog.com*

➡ *Find out if a store website offers better saving options for the same merchandise you wish to buy.*

Left **A nightlife scene, Neighbours** Center **St. Mark's Episcopal Cathedral** Right **Seattle pastime**

Capitol Hill

DISCOVER ONE OF SEATTLE'S *most electrifying neighborhoods on the long ridge that stretches northeast of downtown. The large gay, lesbian, and transgender resident population helped to create a vibrant culture reflected in street scenes that hover on the outside edge of mainstream society. But Capitol Hill is much more than a magnet for self-expression, although you may see more dyed and spiked hair and imaginatively applied body piercings than elsewhere in Seattle. Abundant shops, clubs, restaurants, and cafés along Broadway, Pike and Pine Streets, and 15th Avenue East draw crowds from all over the city. Key attractions include two vintage movie*

Comet Tavern sign

theaters – the Harvard Exit and the Egyptian Theater – the Cornish College of the Arts, the Central Seattle Community College, and the Seattle Asian Art Museum in the sylvan setting of Volunteer Park. There are quiet streets nearby that boast some of the most lavish private residences in Seattle.

🔟 Sights

1 Broadway
2 Pike/Pine Corridor
3 Cathedrals
4 Gay/Lesbian Scene
5 Hendrix Statue
6 Richard Hugo House
7 Volunteer Park Observation Tower
8 Lake View Cemetery
9 Neighborhood Homes
10 Eastlake

On most western Capitol Hill streets, downhill is west, uphill is east. Numbered streets run north-south.

Coffee shops on Broadway

Broadway
If you can buy it, you can find it on Broadway, the nerve center of Capitol Hill. From East Pike to East Roy Streets, store-fronts beckon consumers on the hunt for food, vintage and new clothing, vinyl records, and lots of coffee. On summer evenings especially, the sheer density of pedestrian traffic along Broadway almost matches that of midtown Manhattan. *See pp18–19.*

Pike/Pine Corridor
Bisecting Capitol Hill are two busy streets offering their own flavor and subculture. You can find many of the area's gay and lesbian hangouts on the blocks above and below Broadway, as well as a great selection of taverns and stores selling vintage housewares and furnishings. Although the city has tried to discourage their postings, you may also notice colorful flyers stapled onto telephone poles and virtually any surface, advertising band concerts in the vicinity. If nothing else, they draw attention to the pulse that keeps this community living and breathing on the edge.
🚇 *Map E4*

Cathedrals
Capitol Hill has a number of landmark places of worship, including the grand St. Mark's Episcopal Cathedral, which belongs to the Diocese of Olympia. Organ enthusiasts come from afar to play St. Mark's 3,944-pipe Flentrop organ, installed in 1965. The Saint Nicholas Russian Orthodox Cathedral, one of the oldest parishes of the Russian Orthodox Church outside of Russia, was founded in 1930 by immigrants who fled the 1917 Russian Revolution. The struc-ture's ornate turquoise *lukovitsa* (16th-century "onion dome" style of cupolas) and spires rise high above the trees and neighboring homes. 🚇 *St. Mark's Episcopal Cathedral: Map E4; 1245 10th Ave E • St. Nicholas Russian Orthodox Cathedral: Map M3; 1714 13th Ave*

Gay/Lesbian Scene
Alternative lifestyles are not only tolerated, but encouraged with flagrant same-sex smooching and handholding on the streets. Gay and lesbian clubs *(see p74)* proliferate on the Hill, as do shops selling what used to be called marital aids – sex toys, in today's parlance.

Hendrix Statue

Darryl Smith, an artist once based at the Fremont Fine Arts Foundry, created a lifesize bronze statue of Jimi Hendrix that now graces the Pine Street sidewalk. It shows the musician in his trademark rockstar pose, kneeling in bell-bottoms with his Fender guitar pointed skyward. Before Paul Allen built his EMP Museum *(see pp10 & 32)*, inspired by Hendrix and his music, this installation was Seattle's best-known memorial dedicated to the city's famous guitarist. ◈ *Map M3*

Richard Hugo House

Writers and readers have enthusiastic support from this institution, named for Richard Hugo (1923–1982), a local writer, instructor, and community builder who became one of the most acclaimed American poets of his time. The center advances Hugo's vision by bringing innovative and effective writing programs and workshop education to people of all ages and backgrounds. Visitors are welcome to tour the 16,206-sq-ft (1505-sq-m) Victorian house, built in 1902. ◈ *Map E4 • 1634 11th Ave • (206) 322-7030 • Open noon–6pm Mon–Fri (to 5pm Sat) • www.hugohouse.org*

Seattle Pride March

What began as a protest in 1970 to commemorate the first anniversary of the Stonewall Riots in New York (which sparked the modern gay rights movement), has become a day of unbridled celebration, outlandish pageantry, music, and politicizing. Although Capitol Hill can no longer accommodate the large numbers that come to participate – the rally now takes place in Seattle Center – the Hill remains an important meeting place for Seattle's gay community.

Volunteer Park Observation Tower

Volunteer Park Observation Tower

Built by Seattle's water department in 1906, this 75-ft (23-m) brick tower with an observation deck was designed by the Olmsted Brothers. A short climb of 106 spiraling steps to the deck offers spectacular views of Puget Sound, the Space Needle, and the Olympic Mountains. Volunteer Park is also the site of the Seattle Asian Art Museum *(see p36)* and the Volunteer Park Conservatory. ◈ *Map E4*

Lake View Cemetery

This 1872-era cemetery, on a hilltop just past the northern end of Volunteer Park, is the final resting place for prominent Seattleites, and attracts thousands of visitors each year. Tombstones here identify the pioneers whose names now grace present-day streets or area towns – Denny, Maynard, Boren, Mercer, Yesler, and Renton. Lake View also draws the faithful followers of cinema star and martial arts master, Bruce Lee *(see p31)*, and his son Brandon, whose sculpted tombstones lie side by side. ◈ *Map E3 • 1554 15th E • (206) 322-1582*

 Plant lovers should check out the Volunteer Park Conservatory. Call (206) 684-4743 for information.

Neighborhood Homes

Stroll down the three-block stretch of Denny between Broadway and Olive Way to scout for charming Victorian and Craftsman-style homes and elegant balconies decorated with hanging flower baskets or offbeat art. Marvel at the opulent mansions on the blocks just south of Volunteer Park. Capitol Hill's adjacent Central District, south of Madison and north of 14th Avenue East, is a transitional neighborhood, but features view properties with gorgeous old homes – best seen by car.

Eastlake

An entire neighborhood disappeared when Interstate-5 cut a trough at the base of Capitol Hill. The sliver of a community that remains is called Eastlake, named after the main thoroughfare. Today, it survives as a mixed-use residential community at Lake Union's edge, popular with students, artists, and water-lovers as exemplified by the community of house-boats. REI's flagship store *(see p45)* marks the beginning of Eastlake's commercial area, and farther north, the neighborhood opens up with taverns, cafés, and stores that revel in the geography – halfway between downtown and the University District. ◎ Map E3

Neighborhood home, Denny Way

Up Pine Down Pike

Morning

Begin your late morning promenade at the corner of Pine and Melrose with a strong coffee at **Bauhaus Books & Coffee** *(see p75)*, a longtime Capitol Hill hangout. Walk along Pine (slightly uphill toward Broadway), but make a detour to check out **Le Frock** (613 E Pike St) for bargain top-label and local designers' clothes, or stop at **Area 51** (401 E Pine St), a huge space filled with vintage furniture and kitschy one-of-a-kinds. One block farther east lies **Linda's Tavern** *(see p75)*, a legendary local watering hole frequented by musicians and record label folk that you can scope out for a later visit. Cross Harvard Avenue and you'll notice the vintage **Egyptian Theatre** *(see p39)* on your right, showcasing independent and foreign films.

Afternoon

Cross Broadway, walk four blocks, and turn right on 13th Avenue to Pike Street. Turn right and have lunch at **Elysian Brewing Company** *(see p49)*, home of Seattle's most outstanding pale ale. Walk downhill on Pike to the **Comet** (922 E Pike St), a grungy tavern that's popular with local musicians and wannabes. Cross Broadway and dream about a purchase at **Phil Smart's** (600 E Pike St) for your gold-trimmed imported sports car, or stop by **Babeland** *(see p74)*, a store selling a variety of sex toys. Then grab a cup of coffee and lose yourself in the stacks of one of the city's most popular book-stores, **The Elliott Bay Book Company** *(see p76)*.

Around Town – Capitol Hill

Left **Wildrose** Center **Babeland** Right **R Place**

TOP 10 Gay, Lesbian, Bisexual & Transgender Venues

1 Neighbours
Witness hedonism at its best, with talent shows, wet 'n' wild contests, open mike nights, CD release parties, nightly drink specials, and dancing boys. Thursdays–Saturdays the club stays open for after-hours dancing. ✪ *Map M3 • 1509 Broadway*

2 Wildrose
A lesbian-centric club, although it encourages a mixed and permissive crowd to assemble. The drinks are on the strong side. ✪ *Map M3 • 1021 E Pike St*

3 Re-Bar
The entrance sign perhaps best sums up the philosophy of a club that features some of the area's best DJs: "No minors, drunks, drugs, bigots, or loudmouths." ✪ *Map L3 • 1114 Howell St*

4 The Crescent Lounge
This local dive bar is the current trendy hipster hangout, with entertaining karaoke and reasonably priced drinks. ✪ *Map L3 • 1413 E Olive Way • (206) 720-8188*

5 R Place
Capitol Hill's largest gay club has a full bar and music video monitors on the first floor; dartboards, free pool, and pinball on the second floor; and dancing, live DJs, karaoke, and a weekly strip show on the third floor. ✪ *Map L3 • 619 E Pine St*

6 Eagle
It's Seattle's oldest leather bar, and the atmosphere reeks of a crowd driven by studs and black leather straps and hard rock music. ✪ *Map L3 • 314 E Pike St*

7 The Cuff Complex
An exclusive gay men's club catering to a crowd ranging from 20-somethings to middle agers. Arrive on Sundays for a kegger blowout. ✪ *Map M3 • 1533 13th Ave*

8 Lambert House Gay Youth Center
Organizes activities, support groups, a youth leadership council, dances, and other events to inspire empowerment among 14- to 22-year-olds. The center includes a full kitchen, living room, pool table, library, TV, games, and most important, people who will listen. ✪ *Map E3 • 1818 15th Ave E*

9 Babeland
A store selling sex toys and sponsoring a variety of sex workshops that continue to enlighten, amuse, and shock audiences. ✪ *Map L3 • 707 E Pike St • (206) 328-2914*

10 Lesbian Resource Center
This drop-in center offers help with counseling, job-seeking, and house referrals, as well as information on lesbian events and programs in the area. ✪ *Map B5 • 227 S Orcas St • (206) 322-3953*

 Seattle is one of the most tolerant and liberal cities in the country, and its large gay population compares with San Francisco's.

Left **Bauhaus Books & Coffee** Right **Elysian Brewing Company sign**

10 Cafés & Taverns

1 Victrola Coffee
A real neighborhood café that roasts its own coffee in-house using beans from small farms. The aesthetics reflect music and art of the 1920s and 1930s. ◈ *Map E4 • 411 15th Ave E • $*

2 Bauhaus Books & Coffee
They roast their own coffee here. Drink while you savor the delicious doughnuts and croissants. ◈ *Map L3 • 301 E Pine St • (206) 625-1600 • $*

3 Tavern Law
Hip, stylish speakeasy lounge for young professionals looking to unwind, offering well-made cocktails and thoughtful comfort fare. Try the rich beef-burger. ◈ *Map M3 • 1406 12th Ave • (206) 322-9734 • $$*

4 Caffé Vita
Dark walls and ceilings, wooden floors and tables, and excellent coffee set the tone for this Capitol Hill institution. They roast their own coffee on site; look through the back window to see the apparatus. ◈ *Map M3 • 1005 E Pike St • (206) 709-4440 • $*

5 Remedy Teas
Be spoiled for choice with around 150 types of tea, including blends for hangovers, insomnia, and other ailments. The interior is modern and there is a nice terrace. ◈ *Map E4 • 345 15th Ave • (206) 323-4832 • $*

6 Chop Suey
(See p48).

7 Linda's Tavern
Linda Derschang, a local business owner, created a hip bar for locals in 1994 (who tended to be rock stars and their managers). Mixed drinks, beer, and decent food. ◈ *Map L3 • 707 E Pine St • (206) 325-1220 • $*

8 Hopvine Pub
This neighborhood bar serves handcrafted cask ales from small breweries and serves tasty pub fare. ◈ *Map E4 • 507 15th Ave E • (206) 328-3120 • $$*

9 Comet Tavern
A legendary hangout for rockers and great pretenders alike. It's just a tavern with some pool tables, but the crowd, the location, and the stories etched into tabletops tell a different tale. ◈ *Map M3 • 922 E Pike St • $*

10 Elysian Brewing Company
The chow rates among the best pub grub in town *(see p49).*

By law, bars and taverns check IDs to ensure that customers are 21 or older. Come prepared.

75

Left **The Elliott Bay Book Company** Right **Value Village**

Shops

1 The Elliott Bay Book Company
Peruse the huge selection at this independent bookstore and Seattle institution. It also has a busy café *(see p43)*. Map M3
• 1521 10th Ave • www.elliottbaybook.com

2 Quest Bookshop
As well as over 11,000 titles covering religion, mysticism, and spiritualism, Quest *(see pp18-19)* offers personal astrological charts, tarot decks, audio and visual recordings, and much more.

3 Edie's Shoes
Big spenders and frugal shoppers alike can shop for footwear from chic manufacturers such as Camper, Timberland, and Diesel. Map L3 • 500 E Pike St
• www.ediesshoes.com

4 Value Village
This large thrift store is a Seattle original and has no pretension whatsoever. Items here are not necessarily fashionable, but they are always inexpensive. Map M3 • 1525 11th Ave

5 Harem Off Broadway
From silver jewelry, scarves, and attractive fashions to lovely accents for the home, Harem combines Oriental flair with modern lifestyle. You'll find colorful soft furnishings, furniture, and a range of baskets, candles, and ornaments. The clothing extends to bellydancing outfits. Map M2
• 1715 E Olive Way

6 Pretty Parlor
Stocked with vintage and indie clothing for women, such as dresses and pink tutus, this store is the place to find a unique item for your wardrobe. Map L2 • 119 Summit Ave E • www.prettyparlor.com

7 Martin-Zambito Gallery
Established in 1986, the art gallery specializes in 19th-through 21st-century American and early Northwest Regionalism, with special emphasis on contemporary figurative art, and early women artists. Map L4
• 1117 Minor Ave

8 Wall of Sound
A treasured small, independent shop selling new and rare music CDs and LPs. Carries obscure recordings of rock, jazz, ethnic, electronic, and modern classical, and anything out of the ordinary. Map L3 • 1205 E Pike St

9 Edge of the Circle Books
Seattle's resource for all things pagan and occult. Search for books on Wicca, feng shui, neo-paganism, or ceremonial magic, or purchase your own tarot deck, goblets, and chalices. Map L3 • 701 E Pike St

10 Crypt Off Broadway
A bastion of fetish fashion since the 1980s, the store deals in the latest goth, punk, and industrial fashions. Also sells videos and other accessories. Map M3 • 1516 11th Ave

Some stores will specially order an item not in stock, and ship it to you when it arrives.

Price Categories

Price categories include a three-course meal for one, two glasses of wine and all unavoidable extra charges including tax.

$	under $20
$$	$20–$40
$$$	$40–$55
$$$$	$55–$80
$$$$$	over $80

Garage

🔟 Places to Eat

1 Rancho Bravo Tacos
Colorful, no-frills taqueria, with friendly staff. Loyal customers love the affordable plates of fresh, authentic Mexican fare. ✎ Map M4 • 1001 E Pine St • (206) 322-9399 • $

2 DeLuxe Bar & Grill
Serves an enviable list of brews and better-than-ordinary pub fare in the way of nachos, burgers, and salads. ✎ Map M1 • 625 Broadway E • (206) 324-9697 • $$

3 Quinn's Pub
Popular, upscale bar with dark wood and dim lighting. Guests dine on gourmet burgers and modern American comfort fare. The wild boar Sloppy Joe and house-made sausage with lentils are popular. ✎ Map L3 • 1001 E Pike St • (206) 325-7711 • $$

4 Annapurna Café
This family-run restaurant puts Nepalese, Indian, and Tibetan cuisine under one roof. Choose whichever dumpling, tandoori, or curry item sounds best. ✎ Map M3 • 1833 Broadway • (206) 320-7770 • No wheelchair access • $$

5 Aoki
This longtime Broadway establishment rivals any sushi restaurant in town. Sit at the bar and watch your food being prepared or relax in Aoki's laid-back dining room. ✎ Map M1 • 621 Broadway E • (206) 324-3633 • $

6 Garage
Dodge the crowds at this fine dining, drinking, bowling, and pool-playing place with local rockstar cred. ✎ Map M4 • 1130 Broadway • (206) 322-2296 • $$

7 Pike Street Fish Fry
Youthful, casual eatery where an eclectic crowd stops in to select from a variety of fish and seafood, all fried to perfection and served with tasty home-made sauces like preserved lemon aioli. ✎ Map L3 • 925 Pike St • (206) 329-7453 • $

8 HoneyHole
Find your way down Pike to this heartwarming source of Captiol Hill's hugest and most succulent sandwiches. ✎ Map L3 • 703 E Pike St • (206) 709-1399 • $

9 Via Tribunali
Some of the best authentic Italian pizza in town, with generous, delicious toppings and excellent crusts. ✎ Map L3 • 913 E Pike St • (206) 322-9234 • $$$

10 Lark
Upscale bistro with big plates of Northwest cuisine to share (see p50). ✎ Map M4 • 952 E Seneca St • $$

Unless otherwise noted, all restaurants accept major credit cards and can accommodate vegetarians.

77

Left **Fremont mural** Right *Nouveau* **warehouse architecture**

Fremont

FREMONT DECLARED *itself an "artists'
republic" in the 1960s, when a community of*
students, artists, and bohemians moved in,
attracted by low rents. The name crystallizes
the unflagging spirit of independence,
eccentricity, and most of all,
nonconformity. In retrospect, what may
have begun as an idealistic artists'
enclave was more accurately an early
sign of fast advancing gentrification.
The scenic Lake Washington Ship Canal and
part of Lake Union create its southern border, and
passing boats of all sizes continually refresh the view.
The drawbridge on busy Fremont Avenue rises and falls
deliriously umpteen times a day, snarling traffic that
backs up the hill for blocks. The quaint neighborhood
spawns new boutiques, clubs, and restaurants that keep
changing the face and identity of this town. As Seattle
grows and its population overflows, more and more
professionals seek homes in Fremont, only
minutes away from downtown by car or bus.

**Center of the
Universe signpost**

🔟 Sights

1. Fremont Bridge
2. *Waiting for the Interurban*
3. History House
4. Fremont Ferry & Sunday Ice Cream Cruise
5. Lenin Statue
6. Dinosaur Topiaries
7. Fremont Troll
8. Ship Canal Park
9. Sunday Street Market
10. Outdoor Cinema

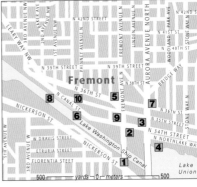

Previous pages **View of Mount Rainier and Lake Union**

History House

Waiting for the Interurban

Fremont Bridge

The lowest of four bridges spanning the Lake Washington Ship Canal, this connects Fremont to residential Queen Anne and two main arterials to downtown. Because of the bridge's low clearance, it faces frequent openings from sailboat, motor yacht, or industrial vessels. Neon art adorns a portion of the span, in the form of a golden-haired Rapunzel and her locks cascading down from the bridgeman's tower. ✪ Map D3 • 3020 Westlake Ave N

Waiting for the Interurban

Frozen in time, Richard Beyer's celebrated 1979 cast aluminum sculpture – five human forms and a dog with a human face – preside at Fremont's busiest intersection, where a community trolley once stopped. Legend has it that the dog's likeness belongs to Arman Napoleon Stepanian, an activist-hero who sparked the recycling movement 30 years ago. The work pokes fun at modern humanity's ennui. It also

represents one of Seattle's earliest public art installations. ✪ Map D2 • N 34th St, Fremont Ave N

History House

Seattle's colorful past is on view at History House where historians interpret and preserve the heritage of the city's distinct neighborhoods. Exhibits in the main gallery complement a three-sided, sepia-tone wall mural that depicts 100 years of Seattle history, encompassing the arts, technology, and industry. Peruse rotating displays of various Seattle neighborhoods. Other features include a sculpture garden and a gift shop.
✪ Map D2 • 790 N 34th St
• (206) 675-8875 • Adm $1 as donation
• www.historyhouse.org

Waiting for the Interurban

Waiting for the Interurban

History House

Fremont Ferry & Sunday Ice Cream Cruise

A labor of love for Captain Larry Kezner, this passenger-only ferry plies the waters of Lake Union from the north shore in Fremont to Lake Union Park on the south shore four times a year. For a more regular service, the Sunday Ice Cream Cruise departs every Sunday on the hour 11am–5pm (in winter from 11am–3pm) from Lake Union Park. ◈ *Map D3* • *(206) 713-8446* • *http://seattle ferryservice.com* • *Adm*

Lenin Statue

Slovakian sculptor Emil Venkov found little interest in his 7-ton (6,350-kg), 25-ft (8-m) likeness of Russian revolutionary V.I. Lenin after the collapse of the Soviet Union. A visiting American, Lewis Carpenter, paid $13,000 for the work and had it shipped through the Panama Canal to his hometown near Seattle. After Carpenter died in 1994, Fremont artist and foundry owner Peter Bevis managed to have the bronze Lenin statue installed in the neighborhood. The incongruity of a Communist icon amidst flourishing shops and capitalist businesses is not lost on anyone. The statue remains a striking symbol that strives to put art before politics. ◈ *Map D2* • *3526 Fremont Avenue N*

Dinosaur Topiaries

Two ivy-covered dinosaur topiaries, which had formerly decorated the lawn near the Pacific Science Center *(see p11)* at Seattle Center, now grace Fremont's narrow Ship Canal Park. To save them from extinction, History House and a group of Fremont artists purchased these in 1999 for $1. The mother, 66 ft (20 m) long, and young apatosauri are now sanctioned by the city and fully integrated into the crazy quilt of what is virtually a neighborhood-wide sculpture garden. ◈ *Map D2* • *Intersection of Phinney Ave & 34th*

Fremont Troll

An icon of Fremont's free spirit is a 15-ft- (4.5-m-) tall Volkswagen-eating troll created by Steve Badanes, Will Martin, Donna Walter, and Ross Whitehead, after winning a national competition sponsored by the Fremont Arts Council *(see p85)*, that in 1989 decided that public art was the best use for a dark space beneath a highway bridge. Though ugly, the troll's location under the north end of Aurora Bridge means that it remains on the route of almost every visitor who walks or takes a tour bus. ◈ *Map D2* • *Intersection of Aurora Ave (Hwy 99) & N 36th St*

Ship Canal Park

A lovely landscaped strip not much wider than a stretch of the Burke-Gilman Trail *(see p84)* attracts tourists all year round. Today, the park creates view-points along the Canal and several places to sit, play chess, picnic, and watch the world go by. Pedestrians don't need to dodge speeding bicycles, however, since there is a separate gravel path for bipeds. ◈ *Map C2* • *Phinney Ave & 2nd Ave NW*

Fremont Troll

Sunday Street Market

Around Town – Fremont

A Morning Around Fremont

Start your picnic with an espresso at **ETG** (3512 Fremont Place N). Cross at the crosswalk just outside the door to 35th Street, turning right to spy the neon-adorned Army surplus missile at 35th and Evanston Avenue N. Turn left on Evanston and walk a block to **PCC** (600 N 34th St), an organic market where you can pick up a delicious carry-out lunch.

Turn left on Evanston for an unobstructed view of the **Ship Canal** and **Fremont Bridge**. Turn right along the Canal path, walk about a block until you see the **Dinosaur Topiaries** at the beginning of the **Ship Canal Park**, a great place for your waterfront picnic. The **Old Trolley Barn** (see p84) is a historic brick building that once housed the **Redhook** microbrewery (see p49). Now it's **Theo Chocolate**, a gourmet chocolate factory. Enjoy the walk down the Canal path, perhaps spotting sailboats or kayakers. When you turn back, exit the park at the topiaries and continue along 35th Street. If you visit during the **Sunday Market**, you'll find blocks of vendors. Continue three blocks to Fremont Avenue, by the Fremont Bridge and the sculpture, *Waiting for the Interurban (see p81)* on a traffic island across the street. Turn left on Fremont Avenue, and get your bearings at the Center of the Universe signpost a half-block later on another traffic island where Fremont Place begins. Stop in **Simply Desserts** (3421 Fremont Ave N) for the richest treats in town.

Sunday Street Market

Rain or shine, the Fremont Sunday Market has withstood the test of time, real estate development, and even lawsuits from neighboring businesses. Begun in 1990 to foster a pedestrian-friendly community and provide an outlet for artists and independent vendors to sell whatever they had to offer, the market hosts up to 200 booths of crafts, imported goods, furniture, food, and knick-knacks that defy description.
⊗ *Map D2 • 34th St • (206) 781-6776 • Every Sunday • Open Apr–Oct: 10am–5pm; Nov–Mar: 10am–4pm • www.fremontmarket.com*

Outdoor Cinema

The *trompe l'oeil* screen and curtains on a factory wall attract hundreds of attendees for campy feature films. It grew from a sparsely attended free affair to a popular summer weekend event that charges admission. Part old-fashioned American drive-in, part Fremont irreverence, people bring their own chairs or sofas and occasionally compete in film-related games between reels. The shows begin after sundown, but audiences begin arriving for the best seats by mid-afternoon.
⊗ *Map D2 • 3501 Phinney Ave • (206) 781-4230 • Every Saturday • Adm • www.fremontoutdoormovies.com*

Aimless walking can be an adventure in Fremont. You just never know who or what will turn up round the next corner.

83

Left **Fremont Bridge with Aurora Bridge towering over it** Right **Adobe Systems building**

🔟 Burke-Gilman Trail Features

1 Bridges
The Burke-Gilman Trail passes under the Fremont Bridge *(see p81)* and the Aurora Bridge. Both span the Ship Canal, although only the draw-bridge opens for boat traffic.

2 Lake Washington Rowing Club
Both athletic teams and individuals hoist their racing shells into the flow from here. The club's nonprofit activities also include training lessons for beginners.
◈ *Map D3 • 910 N Northlake Way*

3 Adobe Systems
A waterfront office building that was designed to leverage the look of Fremont's erstwhile industrial structures houses this software company. ◈ *Map D3*
• 801 N 34th St • (206) 675-7000

4 *Waiting for the Interurban*
(See p81).

5 The Rocket
When an Army surplus store closed in Belltown, its outside adornment ended up in the hands of Fremont sculptors and painters who renovated the World War II-era missile and placed it atop this store.
◈ *Map D2 • 35th & Evanston Ave N*

6 Rope Swing
Sunny days attract a crowd of rope-swingers who get dunked near where Phinney Ave N meets the Canal. ◈ *Map D2*

7 Old Trolley Barn
This large brick warehouse used to house Seattle's early mass transit vehicles, the trolleys. Since then, the building has been, among other things, a microbrewery, and is now a gourmet chocolate factory.
◈ *Map D2 • 34th & Phinney Ave N*

8 Indoor Sun Shoppe
Huge plants decorate the front, and grow lights illuminate the interior of Seattle's favorite neighborhood home and garden store. ◈ *Map C2 • 160 N Canal St*

9 Dock Overlook
The fenced-in area with benches and a roof sits right on the water, making it perfect for sunsets and bird- and boat-watching. Distant views include Salmon Bay's dry-dock industry and the Olympic Mountains beyond to the west. ◈ *Map C2*

10 Gravel Plant
Mounds of gravel, asphalt, and conveyor belts make stark contrast with the solemnity and serenity of the water and park-land nearby. ◈ *Map C2*

The Rocket's lights used to blink as the engine belched smoke every 45 minutes. That mission was eventually aborted.

Fremont Coffee Company

🔟 Fremont Culture

1 First Fridays Art Walk
On the first Friday of each month, art galleries organize self-guided art walks to local studios and establishments including the Fremont Foundry's Gallery and Fremont Coffee Co. ⊗ *Fremont Foundry's Gallery 154: Map C2; 154 N 35th • Fremont Coffee Co.: Map D2; 459 N 36th*

2 Trolloween
A masquerade parade begins its route near the Fremont Troll *(see p82)*. This takeoff on Halloween ends at a bizarre masked ball with lightshows and live entertainment. ⊗ *Map D2 • 36th St N under Aurora Ave*

3 Pumpkin-Carving Contests
During Oktoberfest celebrations, Fremont's brew fest includes the hilarious chainsaw pumpkin-carving competitions.

4 Moisture Festival
This addition to the funky Fremont scene combines elements of Burlesque and carnival for two weeks in spring. Held at the old Hale's Brewery warehouse. ⊗ *Map C2 • 4301 Leary Way NW • www.moisturefestival.com*

5 Fremont Fair
The Solstice Parade *(see p34)*, which includes colorfully clad participants, people-powered floats, and even naked cyclists, kicks off this weekend fair with food, crafts, and music.

6 Summer Park Concerts
Free, family-friendly live music in various parks around Seattle. Check the calendar of events online. In past years, concerts have featured rock, blues, jazz, and folk music. ⊗ *Map D3 • 2101 N Northlake Way • www.summerparkconcerts.com*

7 Fremont Arts Council
Based in an elementary school's 1892-vintage power-house, this community organiza-tion supports creative expression and artists. ⊗ *Map D2 • 3940 Fremont Ave N • (206) 547-7440 • www.fremontartscouncil.org*

8 The Backdoor at Roxy's
This speakeasy lounge has an edgy, baroque style decor. Go for the Fremont fries and the Ryan Gosling cocktail – Rye, Goslings Rum, Crème de Cassis, grapefruit, honey, and lemon, all topped with bubbles. ⊗ *Map C2 • 462 N 36th St • (206) 632-7322 • www.backdooratroxys.com*

9 Glass Art
Dale Chihuly's *(see p37)* influence can be seen in glass studios such as Edge of Glass. ⊗ *Edge of Glass: Map D2; 513 N 36th St*

10 Fremont Library
The city's smallest and most charming library draws the resident literati to spend hours here instead of purchasing the latest author's masterpiece online. ⊗ *Map D2 • 731 N 35th St • (206) 684-4084*

Around Town – Fremont

Around Town – Fremont

Left **Dusty Strings** Right **Ophelia's Books**

Shops

Hub and Bespoke
A bike shop and arty boutique all in one, come here for modern and vintage clothing, and accessories for the hip cyclist. ◎ Map C2 • 513 N 36th St • (206) 547-5730

Dusty Strings
Since 1979, this musical instrument store has attracted players and fans of folk music looking for a levered harp, fiddle, acoustic guitar, or a workshop on hammered dulcimers. ◎ Map D2 • 3406 Fremont Ave N • (206) 634-1662

evo
This sporting goods shop sells a dizzying array of outdoor gear, everything from skis to skateboards, and a variety of active clothing for men and women. It is located in the Fremont Collective, which is also home to the All Together Skatepark (ATS), Seattle's only indoor skatepark. ◎ Map D2 • 3500 Stone Way N • (206) 973-4470 • www.alltogetherskatepark.com

Bellefleur
Fremont lingerie boutique that caters to brides and anyone else who wants to feel pampered and special. ◎ Map D2 • 3504 Fremont Pl N • (206) 545-0222

Les Amis
Window-shoppers find it hard to resist the rustic charm of this women's boutique that stocks designer items by Rozae Nichols, Isabel Marant, Joie, and AG Jeans. ◎ Map D2 • 3420 Evanston Ave N • (206) 632-2877

Frame Up Studios
A simple framing shop which morphed into a lovely and sophisticated resource for one-of-a-kind gift items. ◎ Map D2 • 3515 Fremont Ave N • (206) 547-4657

Show Pony
This well-curated boutique has everything from vintage consignment fashions to clothing from local designers. ◎ Map D2 • 702 N 35th St • (206) 706-4188

Ophelia's Books
Three floors of new and used books, with a large selection of rare and out-of-print editions. ◎ Map C2 • 3504 Fremont Ave N • (206) 632-3759

Fremont Vintage Mall
This underground warren features clothing, furniture, vintage records, knick-knacks, and all sorts of other treasures you never knew you needed. It's easy to while away time here. ◎ Map D2 • 3419 Fremont Place N • (206) 548-9140

Essenza
A fun, funky shop that sells a well-chosen assortment of fine cosmetics, skincare products, perfumes, jewelry, women's lingerie, and more. ◎ Map D2 • 615 N 35th St • (206) 547-4895

86 Discover more at www.traveldk.com

Price Categories

Price categories include a three-course meal for one, two glasses of wine and all unavoidable extra charges including tax.

$	under $20
$$	$20–$40
$$$	$40–$55
$$$$	$55–$80
$$$$$	over $80

Brad's Swingside Café

🔟 Places to Eat

Paseo

1 This busy eatery churns out some of the city's most lauded sandwiches. The most popular are Caribbean Roast and Paseo Press. ◉ *Map D2 • 4225 Fremont Ave N • (206) 545-7440 • No credit cards • $*

Blue C Sushi

2 It's a *kaiten*-style sushi restaurant with a conveyor belt that delivers sushi and teriyaki dinners. Seaweed salad is a surprise hit. ◉ *Map D2 • 3411 Fremont Ave N • (206) 633-3411 • $$*

Uneeda Burger

3 A friendly place serving tasty, upscale burgers and sides such as onion rings. Also on offer are delicious milkshakes and a selection of beer. ◉ *Map D2 • 4302 Fremont Ave N • (206) 547-2600 • $$*

Brad's Swingside Café

4 Chef-owner Brad Inserra enhances his Italian cuisine with flavors from regional US cuisine. A seafood special might include Dungeness crab, Alaskan halibut, locally made sausage, and dishes prepared with exotic African spices. ◉ *Map D2 • 4212 Fremont Ave N • (206) 633-4057 • $$*

El Camino

5 The place for great Mexican preparations using ingredients such as duck, pork adobo, rock shrimp, fresh fish, and chipotle peppers. The margaritas are excellent. ◉ *Map D2 • 607 N 35th • (206) 632-7303 • $$*

Red Door

6 Draws huge crowds for its microbrews and tastefully prepared pub food. The burgers, ribs, salads, and sandwiches are just great. ◉ *Map D2 • 3401 Evanston Ave N • (206) 547-7521 • $$*

Kwanjai

7 You cannot go wrong ordering off the specials board or the regular menu in this Thai restaurant. ◉ *Map D2 • 469 N 36th St • (206) 632-3656 • $*

Qazis

8 One of the best purveyors of classic Indian cuisine that takes no shortcuts. Try the vegetable koftas, lamb korma, tandoori chicken, and *bharta* dishes along with some garlic naan. ◉ *Map D2 • 473 N 36th St • (206) 632-3575 • $$*

Tacos Guaymas

9 This Mexican restaurant offers freshly prepared traditional dishes like *chile rellenos*, quesadillas, and a salsa bar. ◉ *Map C2 • 100 N 36th • (206) 547-5110 • $*

Hale's Ales Brewery

10 Diners sip the latest concoctions brewed in one of Seattle's first authentic brewpubs *(see p49)*.

Unless otherwise noted, all restaurants accept major credit cards and can accommodate vegetarians.

Left **Old brick warehouses in Ballard** Right **Ballard docks**

Ballard

I N THE LATE 19TH CENTURY, *Scandinavian loggers and fishermen established a working waterfront which is still functioning a full century later. Seattle annexed Ballard in 1907, taking advantage of the huge economic growth the mill town fostered; by then Ballard was the state's third largest city. Seattle's commercial fishing fleet resides at Fishermen's Terminal just across Salmon Bay. The late 1990s dot.com boom made real estate prices skyrocket, and scores of boutiques, art galleries, and restaurants opened, reflecting the changing demographics. Popular tourist attractions include the Hiram M. Chittenden Locks and Golden Gardens. The Nordic Heritage Museum celebrates the culture of the area's Scandinavian Americans, and every May 17, the annual Norwegian Constitution Day Parade takes over the streets.*

Bell tower, Ballard

🔟 Sights

1	Nordic Heritage Museum	5	Ballard Avenue
2	Market Street	6	Golden Gardens
3	The Locks	7	Fishermen's Terminal
4	Carl S. English, Jr. Botanical Gardens	8	Sunday Farmers Market
		9	Bardahl Sign
		10	Salmon Bay Industries

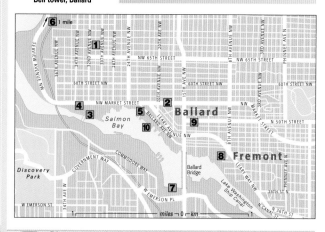

Discover more at www.traveldk.com

Nordic Heritage Museum

With rooms organized by country, this museum illustrates the links between Scandinavian people in the Pacific Northwest. Founded in 1980, it's the only museum in the United States to revere the legacy of immigrants from five Nordic countries – Denmark, Finland, Iceland, Norway, and Sweden. It also enlightens visitors with rotating and permanent exhibits such as colorful Old World textiles, rare china, books and bibles, wood-working tools, and carved wooden ale bowls. There is also a music library. ◈ *Map B1* • *3014 NW 67th St* • *Adm* • *www. nordicmuseum.org*

Market Street

The nerve center of Ballard has a vast selection of stores, cafés, Scandinavian gift shops, and taverns lining both sides of the street. Although Ballard is only about 4 miles (6 km) north-west of Pike Place Market *(see pp8–9)*, the street's melange of local businesses and creative signage reflects the community's small-town personality that has remained intact since the days before Ballard officially became part of Seattle. ◈ *Map B1*

Market Street

Salmon Waves, The Locks

The Locks

Every year, 100,000 vessels pass through the Ship Canal's Hiram M. Chittenden Locks *(see pp20–21)*, and nearly as many tourists come to marvel at the site between Salmon Bay and Shilshole Bay. Named for a retired US Army Corps of Engineers general, the Locks' sophisticated engineering, and the sheer variety of pleasure boats and industrial ships that are able to pass through, impress visitors. The Locks also feature fish ladders to allow migrating salmon to leave from or return to their home streams, best observed between June and November. Don't miss the small but fascinating visitors' center, with its informative short film and displays. ◈ *Map B1* • *7am–9pm daily* • *Visitors' Center: Winter (Oct 1–Apr 30): 10am–4pm Thu–Mon; Summer (May 1–Sep 30): 10am–6pm daily* • *The Army Corps of Engineers offer free guided tours Mar 1–Nov 30* • *(206) 783-7059*

Carl S. English, Jr. Botanical Gardens

Take a little time for a delightful promenade through the greenery of lush trees and rare and exotic plants that fill the garden's seven acres (3 ha), bordering the Locks on the north side of the Ship Canal. The gift shop, which also serves visitors to the Locks, makes a guide available to assist in identifying the plants. ◈ *Map B1* • *3015 NW 54th St* • *9am–7pm daily*

Ballard Avenue

5 From the roaring 1890s through the Great Depression, the four-block stretch of brick-paved Ballard Avenue defines the *raison d'être* of a mill town that also had a thriving boatbuilding and fishing industry. The 19th-century architecture is gorgeous, and it's easy to imagine a street filled with timber millworkers, salty fishermen, fishmongers, and the banks, saloons, and bordellos that served them. In 1976, Sweden's King Carl XVI Gustaf read the proclamation that identified Ballard Avenue as a National Historic District. ✪ Map B1

Golden Gardens

6 Ballard's largest park, and one of Seattle's true urban escapes, includes 87 acres (35 ha) of forested trails, beaches, picnic areas, and great views of Puget Sound and the Olympic Mountains. Originally, the gardens stood at the end of the line for electric streetcars, which were funded by realtors, who wanted Seattle residents to get away from the city's noise and grit. Cool summer nights along the shore bring groups to huddle around bonfires, while sunny days see hundreds of revelers getting tans or playing volleyball in the sand. There is also an off-leash area for dogs, and a boat ramp at the marina. *See p47.*

Golden Gardens

Fishermen's Terminal

Fishermen's Terminal

7 The terminal provides moorage for more than 700 commercial fishing vessels and workboats. Because of the sheltered port and the area's supporting industries and businesses, many Northwest commercial fishermen regard Seattle as the best center for maintenance and repair. The bronze and stone Fishermen's Memorial sculpture, inscribed with the names of more than 500 local men and women, commemorates lives lost during the hard and dangerous work of fishing in Alaska. There are two seafood restaurants on the docks – one's a carry-out with dockside tables. ✪ Map C2 • 3919 18th Ave W

Sunday Farmers Market

8 Like many neighborhoods in Seattle, Ballard attracts weekend shoppers by organizing regional farmers, artists, and craftspeople to fill closed-off streets with an Old World market. The lovely brick pavement and 19th-century architecture along Ballard Avenue form the backdrop for a pleasant walk for the visitors. The market operates year-round, but when summer is in full swing, growers from the arid eastside of the Cascade Mountains bring their

 Although Fishermen's Terminal lies across the Ship Canal from Ballard proper, it is integral to Ballard's identity.

bounty of organic produce, range-fed chickens, and hormone-free beef to sell. 🔍 *Map C2*

Bardahl Sign

Whether you travel by foot, bicycle, car, bus, boat, or plane, the towering, flashing, red neon advertisement for Bardahl automotive oil treatment makes for an unusual icon for any neighborhood. From distant hilltops, the sign's manic ascending flashes harken back to the industrial roots of Ballard, and to company founder Ole Bardahl, Ballard resident and Norwegian immigrant. The sign is one of Seattle's favorite, if most garish, urban landmarks. 🔍 *Map C1*

Bardahl Sign

Salmon Bay Industries

With the opening of the Sinclair Mill in the 1890s, Ballard was given the title "Shingle Capital of the World", as it was instrumental in rebuilding Seattle after the havoc wreaked by the Great Fire of 1889 *(see p30)*. Smaller firms and manufacturers, machine shops, and foundries settled in to stake their claims as well. Today, the area has not changed much. Skirting Ballard's southern waterfront along the Ship Canal, Salmon Bay industries include dry-dock repair and maintenance for ocean-going container ships and barges, and a large gravel company whose equipment dominates the skyline. 🔍 *Map B2*

A Morning Walk Down Ballard Avenue

Begin at the terminus of Ballard Avenue at **Market Street** *(see p89)*. Walk down the west side of the street. Get into gear at **Kavu** (5419 Ballard Ave NW), an independent retailer of active wear that's appropriate for dense woods or dinners out. Cross the street to **Dandelion Botanical Company** (5424 Ballard Ave NW) for natural apothecary items *(see p92)*. Where 22nd Avenue meets Ballard Avenue is a large brick bell tower, rebuilt from the original when Ballard's City Hall tower was destroyed by Seattle's devastating 1965 earthquake. At 5344 Ballard Ave NW, **Horseshoe** entices with a luxurious boutique featuring local and European designer clothing and makeup *(see p92)*. At the next intersection, you'll notice the highly stylized roof crest of the **Ballard Inn** (5300 Ballard Ave NW), which still has "Bank Building" across the top a full century later.

Cross the street. Look for **Tractor Tavern** *(see p48)*, a musical outlet for local and touring musicians who play jazz and country rock. **Second Ascent** *(see p45)* specializes in clothing and gear for budget-minded fans of outdoor recreation. Find a remnant of days gone by at **Dock Street Brokers** (5101 Ballard Ave NW), whose signage matches its early 19th-century structure at 5109 Ballard Avenue. If you're hungry, turn back and stop in **The Other Coast Café** (5315 Ballard Ave NW) for East-Coast-style sandwiches.

Around Town – Ballard

It's best to admire Ballard's industries from a distance. Waterfront car and truck traffic can be hazardous.

Left **LUCCA Great Finds** Right **KuKuRuZa Gourmet Popcorn**

ⁱ⁰Ⱅ Shops

1 LUCCA Great Finds
A rummage in this unique store turns up beautifully restored chandeliers, large old birdcages, antique cards and maps, and colorful candles.
◈ Map B2 • 5332 Ballard Ave NW
• www.luccagreatfinds.com

2 KuKuRuZa Gourmet Popcorn
No ordinary popcorn is sold here. Savory flavors include Jalapeno Cheddar and Buffalo Blue Cheese. Those with a sweet tooth can try Coconut Macaroon or S'mores. ◈ Map B1 • 2211 NW Market St • www.kukuruza.com

3 Me 'n' Moms
This supply store for mothers and children sells cribs, consignment clothes, and imaginative toys at bargain prices.
◈ Map B1 • 2821 NW Market St

4 Horseshoe
Award-winning boutique with a well-chosen collection featuring both local and international designers. The friendly staff adds to the charm (see p91). ◈ Map B1 • 5344 Ballard Ave NW • www.shophorseshoe.com

5 Scandinavian Specialties
The place for all things Scandinavian, with a focus on Norwegian goods. Nordic groceries, sweets, books, household items, and souvenirs are found here.
◈ Map C1 • 6719 15th Ave NW
• www.scanspecialties.com

6 Card Kingdom
Play board games in the café, or choose from the large selection for sale, both classic and unusual. ◈ Map C2 • 5105 Leary Ave NW • www.cardkingdom.com

7 re-souL
This super stylish shoe store is known for its upscale European and American shoes. Also on sale are nifty bags, accessories, and some modern and retro home furnishings. This is a great place to shop for a luxury gift for yourself or someone special. ◈ Map C1 • 5319 Ballard Ave NW • www.resoul.com

8 Secret Garden Bookshop
This small neighborhood bookstore, in business since 1977, has a great selection of new and used books. It also hosts social events and book readings.
◈ Map B1 • 5711 24th Ave NW

9 Camelion Design
An eclectic array of home furnishings, from sofas to lamps to candles, awaits you at this Ballard Avenue contemporary home decor store. ◈ Map C1 • 5330 Ballard Ave NW

10 Dandelion Botanical Company
Opened in 1996, this urban herbal apothecary stocks organic herbs, medicinal oils and tinctures, teas, and bath and body supplies (see p91).
◈ Map B2 • 5424 Ballard Ave NW

Price Categories

Price categories include a three-course meal for one, two glasses of wine and all unavoidable extra charges including tax.	
$	under $20
$$	$20–$40
$$$	$40–$55
$$$$	$55–$80
$$$$$	over $80

Delicious tempting naans, served at India Bistro

🔟 Places to Eat

1 Lockspot Café
This eatery combines American staples at the busy takeout window with a bar and a restaurant inside. ✎ Map B1 • 3005 NW 54th • (206) 789-4865 • $

2 Ray's Boathouse & Café
(See p50).

3 Anthony's HomePort
Diners find excellent service, and fresh seafood that includes king salmon, Dungeness crab, and local oysters. ✎ Map A1 • 6135 Seaview Ave NW • (206) 783-0780 • $$$

4 The Walrus and the Carpenter *(See p51).*

5 Uma
Only steps from Market Street, this small oasis delivers generous portions of popular Thai specialties – authentically flavored, beautifully presented, and at great prices. ✎ Map C1 • 5401 20th Ave NW • (206) 453-5045 • $

6 Hattie's Hat
A great source for huge breakfasts and American rib-sticking dinner standards with a twist: Guinness stout meatloaf, home-made creamed corn, sweet potato fries, and braised southern greens. ✎ Map B1 • 5231 Ballard Ave NW • (206) 784-0175 • $

7 Other Coast Café
Bridge the distance to New York City-style delicatessens by grabbing a sandwich here. Stick to basics such as the reuben with stone-ground mustard or the 12-inch meat or vegetarian subs. ✎ Map B1 • 5315 Ballard Ave NW • (206) 789-0936 • $

8 India Bistro
Relish meat and vegetarian plates prepared in North Indian style. Recommended dishes include spinach or mustard greens with paneer, spicy daal, succulent lamb or chicken tandoori and naan. ✎ Map B1 • 2301 NW Market St • (206) 783-5080 • $$

9 La Carta de Oaxaca
Beeline to this Mexican bistro with tremendous flair, and select from several entrees. The spartan decor is unusual, too – wall art consists of backlit photos of the region where all the flavors originate. ✎ Map B1 • 5431 Ballard Ave NW • (206) 782-8722 • $

10 Salmon Bay Café
This bastion of inexpensive eats attracts blue-collar workers and a large youth crowd. Great four-egg omelets. ✎ Map B2 • 5109 Shilshole Ave NW • (206) 782-5539 • Breakfast & lunch only • $

Unless otherwise noted, all restaurants accept major credit cards and can accommodate vegetarians.

Left **Log House Museum** Center **A coffee shop** Right **Sea stars**

West Seattle

A STRETCH OF ELLIOTT BAY *separates central Seattle from the peninsula of West Seattle, the city's oldest and largest district. Connected by a high freeway bridge and a lower span, West Seattle's proximity to both downtown and the Industrial District has always made it a popular residential area. More than 55,000 people reside here, for since the 1990s dot.com boom West Seattle has attracted a different population of younger, entrepreneurial residents drawn by lower housing costs, the strong sense of community, and some of the best parklands in the city. Alki Beach and its paved waterfront trail brings hordes of revelers when the long, damp winter months give way to sunnier spring days.*

Bill Garnett's West Seattle Ferries mural depicting maritime industry

🔟 Sights

1. Alki Point
2. Constellation Beach
3. The Junction
4. West Seattle Bridge
5. Fauntleroy Ferry Terminal
6. Belvedere Park Viewpoint
7. Log House Museum
8. Camp Long
9. Walker Rock Garden
10. Steel Mill

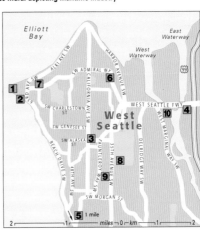

Previous pages **Walker Rock Garden**

Rollerbladers along Alki Beach

Alki Point

Seattle pioneer Arthur A. Denny *(see p30)* and his party aboard the ship *Exact* were the first Europeans to settle the region; they chose the beach-head of West Seattle to come ashore in 1851. Duwamish Tribe Chief Sealth *(see p31)* met the group with open arms and began a long friendship with Seattle's founders. Today, Alki Point boasts row after row of upscale water-front condos for the well-to-do, and a great beach for shell hunting or scuba diving. ◈ *Map A5*

Constellation Beach

Seattle beachcombers check for the year's lowest tides and head to one of the best shoreline secrets, Constellation Beach. It's not the best recreational shore as it lacks a wide sandy stretch, but gets its name from the large numbers of sea stars clinging to the rocky intertidal zone. If the conditions are right, it's not rare to find scores of colorful sea stars, along with the usual anemones, gargantuan sea snails, and geoducks, Puget Sound's giant clams. ◈ *Map A5*

The Junction

The Junction is the epicenter of what used to be an autonomous village in its own right. The name refers to the intersection where California Avenue and Alaska Street meet, and it is here that the bulk of West Seattle's restaurants and shops are located. The small-town feel is palpable as you stroll along California Avenue past mom 'n' pop shops and notice old-timers out for walks or sipping coffee at sidewalk tables. Murals painted on the sides of businesses mirror the warmth and pride of a tightly knit community in its prime, and reflect on its 150-year-old history. Illustrations include the original streetcar lines from 1918. ◈ *Map A6*

West Seattle Bridge

From downtown, the fastest way to anywhere in West Seattle is via this highway, built in 1984. The bridge takes traffic from I-5 and other feeder streets over man-made Harbor Island and the mouth of the Duwamish River, and through to all the major streets in West Seattle. It's visible from many vantage points in town. ◈ *Map B5*

Fauntleroy Ferry Terminal

There's only one ferry from Seattle that gets you to pastoral Vashon Island, and that's the Fauntleroy Ferry with its terminal at the end of Fauntleroy Way. Unlike the downtown terminal, this one is in a residential neighborhood, adjacent to scenic Lincoln Park *(see p47)*. Allow some time to walk along the water's edge to watch ferries come and go. For a memorable visit to Vashon, bring a bike, and look into u-pick berry patches in summer months. ◈ *Map P3*

 Some of the best views of mountains, water, and the city skyline originate from the hilltops in West Seattle.

Belvedere Park Viewpoint

For a bird's-eye view of the city of Seattle and its immediate environment, simply drive or take a bus up Admiral Way to tiny Belvedere Park. Take in 180-degree picture-postcard views of the Cascade Range behind the high-rises of downtown, industrial Harbor Island and the Port of Seattle's container yards, and Elliott Bay and Puget Sound. On clear days, distant and permanently snowcapped Mount Baker on the northeastern horizon looms above all else. If you're in downtown, a 20-minute bus ride to Alki Beach drops you nearby on Olga Street SW. ◈ Map B5
• 3600 Admiral Way SW

Log House Museum

The museum, near Alki Beach, takes local history seriously, as it marks the location where Captain Folger steered his schooner *Exact* in 1851, and brought to the region the families of Seattle's earliest pioneers, the Arthur A. Denny party. The Log House Museum lets you rediscover the history of the Duwamish Peninsula with an orientation center and exhibits that preserve the community's legacy, speaker programs, and special events. ◈ Map A5 • 3003 61st Avenue SW • (206) 938-5293
• Open noon–4pm Thu–Sun • Suggested donation: $3 (adult), $1 (child); tours $2
• www.loghousemuseum.info

Camp Long

In an entirely urban locale, Camp Long comes close to imparting the wild and natural experience usually found only during hikes in local mountain ranges. Once the 1941-era camp served only scouting organizations, but in 1984, the 68-acre (28-ha) compound opened to the

Golf course in Camp Long

general public. Inside the grounds, visitors can hike trails, learn about the environment from professional naturalists, or even rent rustic cabins for in-city camping. One of the most popular attractions is the 20-ft- (6-m-) high Schurman climbing rock, carefully designed to incorporate every climbing maneuver. Bats, opossums, raccoons, chipmunks, and northern flying squirrels have been sighted in the camp. Weekly interpretive walks, rock-climbing classes, and a golf course are also available. ◈ Map B6 • 5200 35th SW • (206) 684-7434

Dredging the Duwamish

Before white settlers landed in what would become Seattle, the Duwamish River zigzagged throughout the valley between the hillsides of West Seattle and Beacon Hill to the east. The area was in many ways more wetland than river until the Army Corps of Engineers dredged it in the late 19th century, deepening the bed and making the Duwamish permanently navigable by commercial vessels. The dredge filled in tideflats to create Harbor Island, which lies between two small channels where the Duwamish pours into Elliott Bay. Many of the port's container yards and maritime industries use this advantageous depot acreage south of downtown.

 Choose your activity based on weather conditions. If it's sunny and warm, head to Alki Beach or take a ferry ride.

9 Walker Rock Garden

Boeing worker Milton Walker failed in his task to create an ornamental concrete lake in his yard between 1959 and 1980. Never one to give up, he redoubled his efforts to create an artistic vision that's outlived the builder. Walker devoted much of his time to sculpting towers, mini-mountains, and trails using countless seashells, crystals, Brazilian agate, and colored glass. Today, the work remains on the private property still owned by his family. ◈ *Map B6 • 5407 37th SW • (206) 935-3036 • By appointment only, June through Labor Day*

Walker Rock Garden

10 Steel Mill

Seattle's remaining steel mill and the city's largest user of electrical power hunkers down on the Duwamish River's western shore. The mill processes recycled scrap from cans, cars, and construction materials just across the river from an upscale yacht marina and office park, embodying Seattle's ethic of mixed-use waterfront. While some may consider the plant an eyesore and major polluter, it competes successfully with Asian firms and provides jobs for the local economy. ◈ *Map B5*

A Morning at Alki Beach

Experience the scenic Alki Avenue via a leisurely walk and easy bike ride along a waterfront trail (about 3.5 flat miles – 5.5 km – each way). Begin at the **Coast Guard Station** (3201 Alki Ave) which offers tours of the Alki Point lighthouse on weekends from June to August (1:30–4:30pm). Walking northeast, stop at 63rd Ave SW to see a monument erected to celebrate the arrival of Seattle's early settlers. At 61st Ave SW, just before **Alki Beach Park** begins, look for the miniature **Statue of Liberty** on the right, built in 1952 on the strip of land dubbed "New York Alki" by the early settlers.

The sandy stretch of Alki Beach begins around 60th Ave. Stroll until 53rd Ave while taking in the views of Puget Sound, its ships and sailboats to the north, and the **Olympic Mountains** to the west. Rent a beach bike nearby at **Wheel Fun Rentals** (2530 Alki Ave SW) and continue along the trail. **Public restrooms** are available at the intersection of 57th Ave SW. As the road curves and becomes Harbor Ave, have a look through the telescopes set up above the seawall for more great views. Near the 1100 block of Harbor Ave you'll notice **Don Armeni Park**, where wedding parties and professional photographers often congregate to snap pictures of the city skyline. Stop at **Salty's on Alki Beach** (see p101) for a seriously scrumptious Sunday brunch that includes an all-you-can-eat Dungeness crab and other seafood indulgences.

Parking is extremely hard to find at Alki in summer. Consider taking a bus, biking, or walking from a short distance away.

Avalon Glass Works

🔟 Shops

1 Avalon Glass Works
Watch artists create blown-glass vases, bowls, sculpture, ornaments, garden floats, paperweights, and seasonal items in myriad shapes, colors, and sizes in this exciting workshop.
Ⓢ *Map B5 • 2914 SW Avalon Way*

2 Carmilia's
Along with assorted jewelry and accessories for women, the boutique sells apparel manufactured by Nanette Lepore, Ella Moss, and Hanky Panky. Ⓢ *Map A6 • 4528 California Ave SW*

3 West Seattle Computers
The technical staff at this computer store are as friendly as they are savvy. You can buy software or hardware, or solve problems with whatever digital personal assistants you may have.
Ⓢ *Map A6 • 4522 California Ave SW*

4 Metropolitan Market
This neighborhood super-market and gourmet purveyor of prepared food offers customized salads, pasta dishes, and *panini* (grilled sandwiches) cooked to order, and creative side dishes galore. The store also sells quality kitchenware. Ⓢ *Map B5 • 2320 42nd Ave SW • $*

5 Pharmaca Integrative Pharmacy
Professional and personalized service focuses on wellness at this pharmacy. Ⓢ *Map A6 • 4707 California Ave SW*

6 Clementine
This tiny shoe boutique specializes in European and Brazilian shoes for women. There is also a nice selection of jewelry by local designers, as well as handbags and accessories.
Ⓢ *Map A5 • 4447 California Ave SW*

7 Easy Street Records
Shop here for the latest in Indie Rock, then stop off for lunch and an espresso in the café.
Ⓢ *Map A6 • 4559 California Ave SW • www.easystreetonline.com*

8 Northwest Art & Frame
This welcoming store offers an enormous selection of custom and ready-made frames, while also selling a variety of art supplies, cards, stationery, and gift items. Ⓢ *Map A6 • 4733 California Ave SW*

9 Curious Kidstuff
Find all manner of tricks and treasures for children at this fun and welcoming toy store. There is a large selection of non-violent, eco-green, and wooden toys.
Ⓢ *Map A6 • 4740 California Ave SW • www.curiouskidstuff.com*

10 JF Henry Cooking & Dining
This is the best resource for quality china, silver and stainless flatware, and crystal. The store carries hundreds of patterns displayed beautifully with great discount offers. Ⓢ *Map A6 • 4445 California Ave SW • www.jfhenry.com*

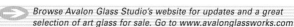

Browse Avalon Glass Studio's website for updates and a great selection of art glass for sale. Go to www.avalonglassworks.com

Price Categories	
Price categories include a three-course meal for one, two glasses of wine and all unavoidable extra charges including tax.	**$** under $20 **$$** $20–$40 **$$$** $40–$55 **$$$$** $55–$80 **$$$$$** over $80

Luna Park Café

Places to Eat

1 La Rustica
Dine on exquisite Italian classics such as spaghetti with garlic, prawns, polenta, or pizza with mushrooms and prosciutto. ✪ *Map A5 • 4100 Beach Drive SW • (206) 932-3020 • $$$*

2 Phoenecia
Come to Phoenecia to enjoy delicious tapas, gourmet pizzas, or wonderful lamb dishes. In summer you can dine outside, with lovely views of the beach. ✪ *Map A5 • 2716 Alki Ave SW • (206) 935-6550 • $$*

3 Luna Park Café
Inside, the decor and kitschy artifacts reflect the style of the 1950s. Popular basics include the BLT and club sandwiches, hand-dipped malted milkshakes, and spinach salad. ✪ *Map B5 • 2918 SW Avalon Way • (206) 935-7250 • $*

4 Azuma Sushi
Insiders return often for their fix of professionally prepared sushi and sashimi, sake, and teriyaki at very reasonable prices. ✪ *Map A6 • 4533 California Ave SW • (206) 937-1148 • $$*

5 Bakery Nouveau
This award-winning bakery always has queues for its inviting assortment of fresh, buttery, flaky treats. A friendly staff also serves gourmet coffee drinks and delicious pizza to devoted local crowds. ✪ *Map A6 • 4737 California Ave SW • (206) 923-0534 • $*

6 Mission
Head to Mission for Latin American food and great margaritas. ✪ *Map A5 • 2325 California Ave SW • (206) 937-8220 • $$*

7 Jak's Grill
This steakhouse prepares superb beef, chicken, and fish dishes, and the price includes several side orders. ✪ *Map A6 • 4548 California Ave SW • (206) 937-7809 • $$*

8 Salty's on Alki Beach
Specials reflect the freshest seasonal fish and seafood, and picture windows offer diners the most breathtaking views of Elliott Bay. ✪ *Map B5 • 1936 Harbor Ave SW • (206) 937-1600 • $$$*

9 Chelan Café
Dine on typical American truck-stop fare; burgers, fries, meatloaf, or eggs. ✪ *Map B5 • 3527 Chelan Ave SW • (206) 932-7383 • $*

10 West 5
Munch on comfort food like BLTs and burgers at this hip eatery. ✪ *Map A6 • 4539 California Ave SW • (206) 937-1966 • $$*

→ Following pages **Cafés on Pier 56, Elliott Bay**

STREETSMART

Planning Your Trip
104

Getting to Seattle
105

Getting Around Seattle
106

Things to Avoid
107

Budget Tips
108

Special Needs
109

**Banking &
Communications**
110

Security & Health
111

Shopping Tips
112

**Eating &
Accommodation Tips**
113

Places to Stay
114-119

SEATTLE'S TOP 10

Left **Seattle's Convention & Visitors Bureau** Right Maps

🔟 Planning Your Trip

1 Tourist Offices
Seattle's Convention & Visitors Bureau can provide information for organizing a visit to Seattle, and Washington State Tourism is helpful for information on the rest of the state.

2 Media
Seattle has one major daily newspaper, covering current events and vital information, the *Seattle Times*. The Thursday and Friday editions include additional entertainment sections. The *Seattle Post-Intelligencer* (www.seattlepi.com) offers similar information, but is only available online. Two public radio stations, KUOW (FM) and KEXP (FM), broadcast programs based on news, current affairs, and pop music.

3 Internet
Many Internet users have their own favorite travel sites, and the web has almost infinite resources for everyone. Websites with a wealth of information on Seattle include www.seattle.gov and www.visitseattle.org.

4 Maps
Seattle's streets are arranged in a typical American-style grid. It's best to familiarize yourself with Seattle's layout, however, as bodies of water and steep hills create plenty of curves and cul-de-sacs. Pick up free maps at most tourist bureaus and attractions.

5 Insurance
It's wise, if not essential, to take out travel insurance before you travel. Policies can cover canceled flights or cruises and lost baggage in addition to medical expenses. If you have health insurance at home, save receipts from any medical expenses incurred during your trip.

6 When to Go
July is historically the driest month of the year, and late spring, summer, and early fall are the most mild and appealing times to visit. Most festivals and street fairs occur during the summer months. Be prepared for rain in fall, winter, and early spring.

7 What to Take
Seattle championed the informal look, so bring casual, all-purpose clothes. Winters can be cold and some summer nights cool right down, so a sweater or jacket is a necessity. An umbrella is handy year-round.

8 How Long to Stay
A week should allow plenty of time to take in the main attractions and to take a day trip or two. Two weeks would allow a more comprehensive experience in Seattle, as well as in its scenic surrounding areas.

9 Visas
Canadian citizens need proof of nationality to clear United States Customs. Australian, Japanese, New Zealand, and most European citizens must apply well in advance (and pay a fee) for entry clearance via the Electronic System for Travel Authorization (ESTA). See https://esta.cbp.dhs.gov for more details. Other nationalities must secure a visa from a US consulate or embassy prior to travel.

10 Embassies
Every country has an official diplomatic representative from the United States. Contact the US embassy or consulate in your country if you have any queries about current visa requirements.

Directory

Seattle's Convention & Visitors Bureau
www.visitseattle.org
www.seattle.gov

Washington State Tourism
www.experience wa.com

Seattle Times
www.seattletimes.com

Seattle Post-Intelligencer
www.seattlepi.com

KUOW 94.9 (FM)
www.kuow.org

KEXP 90.3 (FM)
www.kexp.org

For more information on embassies and consulates **See p111.**

Left **Seattle-Tacoma International Airport** Right **Amtrak**

Getting To Seattle

1 Seattle-Tacoma International Airport

Sea-Tac Airport (SEA) lies about 10 miles (16 km) south of Seattle. The main terminal leads out to the road where taxis and buses collect passengers. If you arrive at the north or south satellite terminals, you must first take a subway to the main terminal. ⓢ *Map P3*

2 Customs

Federal law allows each visitor to bring in $100 worth of gifts, 1 liter of liquor, and 200 cigarettes duty-free. Cash or negotiable funds exceeding $10,000 must be declared.

3 Left Luggage

You may store your luggage at Ken's Baggage and Frozen Food Storage at Sea-Tac Airport, located on the Baggage Claim level between carousels 12 and 13.

4 Lost Property

Sea-Tac Airport operates a Lost and Found service in the central part of the main terminal. You can also contact your airline for items left on an airplane.

5 Shuttles, Buses & Light Rail

Shuttles stop at all major downtown hotels. Central Link light rail operates a service from Sea-Tac to downtown Seattle, which takes 37 minutes and costs $2.75. Check if your hotel reservation includes a free shuttle from the airport; otherwise, look for Sea-Tac's Ground Transportation Information Booth.

6 Taxi or Limousine

Yellow Cab is the only taxi company authorized to take passengers from the airport, although any carrier can bring you to the airport. Fares to downtown cost about $32 and take about 15 minutes, not including a suggested 10 percent tip. Private limousine services are more costly.

7 Portland International Airport (PDX)

Only a few miles outside of central Portland, Oregon, PDX is a distant alternative on the way to or from Seattle. It's possible to catch an Amtrak train to Seattle from Portland, sometimes for only $41 one way.

8 Kenmore Air

Visitors from Victoria and the Gulf Islands, British Columbia, can make the memorable trip to Seattle on a seaplane that lands on Lake Union.

9 Greyhound

There are four Greyhound bus services every day from San Francisco to Seattle, but the journey takes almost 24 hours.

10 Amtrak

Seattle's King Street Station is the depot for Amtrak passenger trains from Vancouver, British Columbia, and all points south and east. Find the entrance in between Pioneer Square and the International District. The Coast Starlight rides the rails between Los Angeles and Seattle daily, and Amtrak *Cascades* itineraries include towns and cities between Eugene, Oregon, and Vancouver, BC.

Directory

Airports
- SEA: (206) 787-5388; www.portseattle.org/seatac
- PDX: (877) 739-4636; www.flypdx.com
- Kenmore Air: 1-866-435-9524; www.kenmoreair.com
- Ken's Baggage & Frozen Food Storage: www. kensbaggage. com

Bus
- Greyhound Ticket Center: 1-800-231-2222; www.greyhound.com

Train
- King St Station: 1-800-872-7245; www. amtrak.com

Shuttle
- Shuttle Express: (425) 981-7000; www. shuttleexpress.com

Metsker Maps of Seattle has a thorough inventory of maps (**see p69**). *Call them at (206) 623-8747 or 1-800-727-4430.*

Left **A Seattle bus stop sign** Center **Seattle taxi cab** Right **Seaplane**

Getting Around Seattle

Buses
Metro Transit offers the most inexpensive transportation. A single journey off-peak costs $2.25; peak times, it's $2.50–$3. Exact fare is required. Pay on entry for buses heading downtown, and on leaving for buses heading away from downtown. Ask the driver for a free transfer if you are connecting with another bus. Most buses these days are equipped with wheelchair lifts.

Ferries
For a sensorial way to experience Seattle and its environs, consider taking a ferry. Major routes include: Seattle-Winslow (on Bainbridge Island) and Seattle-Bremerton from Pier 52; and West Seattle-Vashon Island and West Seattle-Southworth from the Fauntleroy terminal. From Anacortes, some distance north of Seattle, there is ferry service to the San Juan Islands and Sydney (on Vancouver Island, north of Victoria).

Water Taxis
Daily water taxis operate between Pier 55 and Seacrest Dock in West Seattle. The journey takes around 12 minutes and costs $4 each way prepaid, $4.75 cash.

Taxis
Seattle has abundant licensed taxi operators, and you can flag them down from most downtown streets. You can also call to book a cab by phone.

Seaplane
Kenmore Air *(see p105)* has a large fleet of seaplanes offering tours to sightsee Puget Sound, the Olympic Mountains, and the Cascade Range.

Car
Driving in Seattle can be a challenge due to large volumes of traffic on downtown streets, freeway logjams, and alternating one-way streets that seem to baffle many drivers.

Boat
You can rent canoes and kayaks, or sailboats and fishing boats with or without crews. A number of companies on the waterfront, such as Argosy Cruises, provide tours on Elliott Bay, Lake Union, and Lake Washington.

Motorbike
Motorbikes and gas or electric scooters provide more freedom and use far less fuel than the average car. Try renting one for an exciting way to explore Seattle's hilly terrain.

Bicycle
Cyclists are a lot safer on paths reserved for non-motorized vehicles. There is a city-wide bicycle helmet law.

Commuter Rail
Seattle's commuter rail service, Sounder, links Seattle's King Street Station with Everett, Edmonds, Puyallup, Sumner, Auburn, Kent, Tukwila, and Tacoma. Service is quite limited, though; check the relevant schedule for times. A light-rail service links downtown Seattle with Sea-Tac Airport.

Directory

Buses
• Metro Transit Rider Information: (206) 553-3000; http://metro.king county.gov

Ferry
• Washington State Ferries: (206) 464-6400; www.wsdot.wa.gov/ferries

Car Rentals/Taxis
• American Automobile Association: (206) 448-5353; http://www.aaa.com

Motorbikes
• Mountain to Sound Motorcycle Adventures: (425) 222-5598; www.mtsma.com

Bicycles
• Gregg's Greenlake Cycles: (206) 523-1822
• Wheel Fun Rentals: (206) 932-2035 • Maps: www.seattle.gov/transportation/bikemaps.htm

Commuter Rail
• Sounder: 1-888-889-6368; www.sound transit.org

 Call Argosy Cruises to see Seattle from the waterfront. Harbor cruises start at around $24. Tel: 1-888-623-1445.

Left **Traffic sign for pedestrians** Center **No smoking sign** Right **Waterproof windbreaker**

10 Things to Avoid

1 Don't Call it the Emerald City
This name derives from Seattle's rain-soaked greenery and once heavily forested ecology. But locals certainly do not refer to their home that way, although occasionally you may hear Seattle called Jet City, a reference to Boeing's influence on the economy.

2 Don't Jaywalk
Jaywalkers often find themselves collared by waiting police patrols on the lookout for any pedestrian crossing the street at unauthorized places or times. Police do enforce the statute that makes crossing against the light illegal.

3 Yield to Pedestrians
Seattle has a history of protecting pedestrians from collisions with automobiles. All motorized and self-powered vehicles riding the streets have an obligation to stop for pedestrians, whether or not they cross at intersections or outside of crosswalks.

4 Unsafe Neighborhoods
Most tourists never come near the edgier neighborhoods where economic disenfranchisement has helped to foster street crime. Seattle's major streets and arterials are quite safe for sightseeing during the day. Feel free to stroll at night only if you already know the area comfortably.

5 Smoking
Smoking is prohibited in all public places in Washington, including in hotels. It is also an offence for smokers on the street to smoke within 25 ft (7.6 m) of any doorway, window, or air vent. This rule is designed to prevent employees from standing outside their place of work to smoke. Businesses caught violating the rule incur a $100 fine.

6 Driving Challenges
One's patience is tested when navigating Seattle's streets and highways. Keep a lookout for turn-only lanes at busy intersections. If you need to parallel-park on steep hills, turn your wheels towards the curb to help prevent a runaway car. If you use manual transmission and you're stopped in traffic mid-hill, be sure to apply the emergency brake until you engage the gears smoothly. You must obey the speed limits, 25 mph (40 km/h), unless posted otherwise.

7 Underdressing
Seattle has two main seasons, wet and dry. Regardless of the time of year, always remember to pack a jacket or sweater, and basic rain gear. Waterproof windbreakers, hats, or polypropylene shells are essential.

8 Panhandlers & the Homeless
All cities have an abundance of homeless individuals, and Seattle is no exception. Avoid contact with panhandlers and beggars and those that are obviously intoxicated. They're rarely aggressive, but it's still a good idea to ignore confrontation. Always keep your possessions firmly in hand or secure.

9 Forgetting to Tip
Almost every restaurant's management keeps wages very low and expects customers' tips to make up the difference. Your gratuity should be in the 15–20 percent range, more or less depending on the quality of service, and calculated on the pre-tax total. Tip your cab driver 10–15 percent, and allow about $1 per service for hotel staff.

10 Age Restrictions & ID
The legal drinking age for alcoholic beverages is 21. The law is so strictly enforced that everyone's picture identity card is checked at bars and taverns regardless of how old they may look. Be prepared to show proof of age. You must be 18 or older in order to purchase cigarettes.

 Parking meters downtown cost $2–$4 per hour, depending on location. If you must drive, look for a parking garage or lot.

Left **Pike Place Market** Right **CityPass ticket**

🔟 Budget Tips

1 Discount Air Tickets

You can uncover outstanding rates on the Internet. But be sure to call reservation numbers and search the websites of major airlines along with your forays into third-party travel sites to discover the most advantageous deals.

2 Hotel Deals

Hotel rates are subject to pricing grids based on such criteria as special promotions, high- and low-season rates, and room categories. Use your intuition: if something sounds impossibly low, it probably should not be trusted. Call the hotel directly and ask for the best price after researching wholesalers and even the hotel's own website *(see pp114–19)*.

3 Fly-Drive Packages

If you stay in or close to downtown and have no plans to explore the surrounding region, you will not need a car. But if you want to spread your wings, many fly-drive packages have built-in price advantages over renting a car separately.

4 Discount Coupons

Avoid waiting in long lines and get one universal pass online. You may purchase a CityPass online or at the first attraction you visit. Valid for nine days, the pass includes admission to Woodland Park Zoo, the Space Needle, Pacific Science Center, Seattle Aquarium, the Museum of Flight, EMP Museum, and Argosy Cruises.
🕲 www.citypass.com

5 Cheaper Sleeps

The central location of Seattle's hostels combined with exceptionally low rates is too irresistible to ignore. Hostelling International, featuring a lounge, library, and self-service kitchen/laundry, and Green Tortoise Hostel *(see p118)* are decent places to stay.
🕲 *Hostelling International: www.hiseattle.org*

6 Cheaper Eateries

Cheap eats are widely available. Look anywhere in the International District, especially in the Vietnamese areas, for dinners under $7. Taquerias and sandwich delis dot corners in every neighborhood, and Indian restaurants offer all-you-can-eat lunch buffets.

7 Picnics

The Pike Place Market *(see pp8–9)* is a great place to shop for a picnic in one of the city's many parks. Try DeLaurenti's or Three Girls Bakery for easily portable breads, sandwiches, salads, and freshly baked pastries.

At Greenlake, purchase delicious organic carry-out food at PCC Natural Markets.
🕲 *PCC Natural Markets: Map P2 • 7504 Aurora Ave N • (206) 525-3586*

8 Public Transport Passes

Seattle has no rapid transit system, but you can use the Metro bus system. Purchase multiple ticket booklets of various dollar values from major bus stations or from Safeway, Bartell Drugs, or QFC stores. Call Metro Transit Rider Information *(see p106)*.

9 Communications

It may be a good idea to purchase a prepaid phone card before you leave home. Most of Seattle's branch public libraries offer free Internet access at their computer stations.
🕲 *Seattle Public Library: Map K5 • 1000 4th Ave • (206) 386-4636 • www.spl.org*

10 Laundromats

These have largely been relegated to lower income neighborhoods in a city that's on the expensive side. University Laundry Center operates a coin-operated laundromat in the U-District. Check online for other laundromats near where you are staying. 🕲 *University Laundry Center: Map E2 • 4522 Brooklyn NE • (206) 853-6522*

Left **Sign to help disabled travelers** Center **Braille Institute of Seattle** Right **Student's ID**

Special Needs

1 Designated Parking

You may park in specially designated spaces if you are disabled and have the proper vehicle identification clearly posted. Any unauthorized use may cause a traffic infraction with a $250 penalty.
§ *Department of Licensing: (306) 902-3900*

2 Special Prices

Seattle's Metro Transit system and many other attractions offer discounted fare for senior citizens and the disabled. The Regional Reduced Fare Permit costs $3 and entitles you to reduced fares on Metro Transit, Washington State Ferries, Community Transit, and Sound Transit. Visitors wishing to obtain such a pass will need an American Disabilities Act (ADA) paratransit card. National parks also issue special vehicle passes for the disabled that entitle all passengers in the vehicle to enter for free.
§ *ADA: 1-800-514-0301*
• *Metro Rider Information: (206) 553-3000*

3 Required Accessibility

Any new construction in Seattle must conform to the ADA by providing easy access for the disabled in wheelchairs. While newer hotels and restaurants will by law have met the requirements, you need to call in advance to inquire if

your destination has conformed to the emerging standards.

4 "Kneeling" Buses

Seattle's Metro system pioneered the use of Lift-U lifts on public transportation buses to accommodate those who use wheelchairs or have difficulty using stairs. Look for a wheelchair symbol posted next to the scheduled arrival times on placards posted at bus stops.

5 Ramped Curbs

Every downtown corner provides ramped curbs, and frequent neighborhood street construction entails installing ramps where they do not already exist. Most government buildings, supermarkets, tourist attractions, performance venues, and hotels have clearly marked hands-free entrance and egress doorways and ramps.

6 Accessible Toilets

Seattle has an exemplary record of providing disabled access to toilets in public restrooms. However, public restrooms for the general public are few in Seattle, although there are public washrooms at the Pike Place Market.

7 Visually Impaired Travelers

Founded in 1965, the Community Services for the Blind and Partially

Sighted is a great resource for sight-impaired individuals. The Seattle Public Library offers a Washington Talking Book & Braille Library and an equal access library program.
§ *Community Services for the Blind & Partially Sighted: 1-800-458-4888*
• *Washington Talking Book & Braille Library: 1-800-542-0866; www.wtbbl.org*

8 Gay & Lesbian Travelers

Seattle has many organizations that assist gay, lesbian, bisexual, and transgender travelers with gender-related information. The *Seattle Gay News* is widely available. § *Pride Foundation: (206) 323-3318; www.pridefoundation.org*
• *Seattle Gay News: www.sgn.org* • *PFLAG: (206) 325-7724; www.seattle-pflag.org* • *Lesbian Resource Center: (206) 322-3953; www.lrc.net*
• *Lambert House (see p74)*

9 Children's Needs

When traveling with children, be aware of their tired and sore feet, boredom, and short attention spans. Always pack a few snacks and essential medications.

10 Students

Use your student ID card for reduced admission to museums, festivals, gallery events, concerts, and other special programs.

Be wary of downtown public restrooms as they are often havens for unsavory activity.

Left **ATM** Center **US Post Office** Right **Coin-operated pay phone**

🔟 Banking & Communications

1 Exchange
Look for currency exchange offices in the main terminal and South Satellite at Sea-Tac Airport (see p105), and at major banks downtown. Travelex has an exchange branch at 4th Avenue and Pine as well. You can avoid bad rates by obtaining cash from ATMs, where daily rates are more advantageous.

2 ATMs
You may incur a small fee for using the ATM if you are not a customer of the bank (your own bank may charge you, too). Check with your bank for charge rates before you travel.

3 Credit Cards
Rental car agencies and hotels require a credit card for booking reservations. While many smaller eateries still do not accept cards, the majority of restaurants do. Call the bank's toll-free number if you lose your card. Always keep a small amount of cash for tips and small purchases.

4 Traveler's Checks
The use of debit and credit cards has made traveler's checks less popular. Their face value is equal to cash if you buy them in dollars, but you need to present a photo ID, and cashing

them in banks or currency exchange offices can be time-consuming.

5 Currency
The US currency is the dollar, and one dollar is made up of 100 cents. Visitors from outside the US should become familiar with the currency in advance. The counterfeit-proof bills can be difficult to distinguish from each other.

6 Tax
Most restaurants charge 10 percent sales tax, while retail purchases are subject to a combined state and city sales tax of 9.5 percent. Car rentals at the airport include sales tax, an additional 10 percent tax, plus the 10 percent airport concession fee – 28.3 percent above initial rental price.

7 Post Offices
Most post offices operate Monday to Friday from 9am to 5pm; some branches open on Saturdays from 9am for 3–6 hours, depending on their location.

8 Telephones
Seattle's area code is 206, but the vastness of surrounding suburbs has necessitated several prefixes. 425 covers most of the Eastside (see pp54–5), 253 covers south of the city, and 360 handles outlying areas. Local calls made

from Seattle to those other areas require that you dial 1, the area code, and the seven-digit number. Toll-free numbers begin with 800, 877, or 888. Dial 411 for directory assistance, 011 for an international call, and 911 in case of an emergency.

9 Internet
There's no shortage of coffee shops, cafés, and Internet cafés in Seattle, most of which offer high-speed and free Wi-Fi service for seamless remote and wireless connections laptop users. Seattle public libraries (see p108) offer free Internet access, though time limits sometimes apply.

10 Courier Services
The most popular overnight services are FedEx, UPS, and DHL (international deliveries only). Also consider using the competitively priced services of the United States Post Office for overnight, second-, or third-day guaranteed deliveries.

Directory

Travelex
1-800-287-7362

Express & Courier Mail
• *FedEx: 1-800-463-3339*
• *UPS: 1-800-742-5877*
• *DHL: 1-800-225-5345*

You may find the relatively rare $2 bill or a $1 coin in circulation in the US, but the former has virtually disappeared from use.

Left **A park ranger** Center **Hospital facade** Right **Compact first-aid kit**

⁝⁰10 Security & Health

1 Earthquake Procedures

Should an earthquake strike, stay calm. If you are indoors, stand under a load-bearing doorframe or get under a heavy desk or table. If you're driving, stay in the vehicle and park in an open area away from lamp posts and bridges. Major earthquakes are extremely rare, although the Puget Sound region includes several fault-lines that are susceptible to temblors.

2 Consulates

Most major countries have consulates in the city. If anything untoward occurs, contact your national representative.

3 Petty Crime

Every city has problems with petty crime, especially for tourists who may look lost. The best defense is to be aware of your surroundings. Don't walk into any area that looks questionable.

4 Emergencies

Dial 911 from any phone during an emergency. Be prepared to provide your location and the circumstances to the aid dispatcher so that the appropriate help will arrive quickly.

5 AIDS

The AIDS virus is still a public health problem, so don't take risks engaging in unprotected sex. Seattle has ample public health facilities and centers that offer free services.

6 Helplines

Find support and information for almost any problem via Seattle's public service helplines.

7 Police Reports

If you are the victim of a crime, you should report it to the nearest police department as soon as possible. You will be issued a police report, which will be needed for any insurance claims you make.

8 Outdoor Safety

Ask any staffer working at a reputable outdoor recreation store for general information about a particular area. Ranger stations are also excellent sources for information. Even for a day hike, you'll want reserves of food, water, spare seasonal clothing, and first aid, among other personal items.

9 Hospitals & Clinics

Seattle has an enviable list of first-rate medical institutions that provide emergency care, health-care services, and treatment, including Harborview Medical Center (Seattle's public hospital), Swedish Medical Center, and Virginia Mason Medical Center.

10 Health Insurance Claims

You should plan on paying for any health care at the time of (or even before receiving) treatment. Save receipts for reimbursement by your insurance company. Prevent billing worries by confirming in advance that the hospital or clinic you choose accepts your form of coverage.

Directory

Consulates
• Australia: (206) 575-7446; austemb.org
• Canada: (206) 443-1777; http://can-am.gc.ca/seattle
• New Zealand: (310) 566-6555; www.nzcgla.com
• UK: (415) 617-1330; www.gov.uk/government/world/usa

AIDS
• Washington State HIV/AIDS Hotline: 1-800-272-2437

Helplines
• Washington Poison Center: 800-222-1222
• Crisis Clinic: (206) 461-3222
• Sexual Assault Hotline: (800) 562-6025

Hospitals & Clinics
• Harborview Medical Center: (206) 744-3000
• Swedish Medical Center: (206) 386-6000
• Virginia Mason Medical Center: (206) 223-6600

Leave home with a clear understanding of how your health insurer handles payments and/or reimbursements.

Left **Sunday Street Market, Fremont** Right **Market Street, Ballard**

🔟 Shopping Tips

1 Department Stores

Although suburban shopping malls have the bulk of nationally recognized chain department stores, downtown shopping opportunities serve the needs of Seattle's residents in a variety of ways. Find most of the larger stores, such as Nordstrom's flagship store and Macy's, centered in the Westlake Plaza area between 4th and 5th Avenues and Pike and Stewart Streets (see pp52–3).

2 Boutiques

Discover one-of-a-kind designer wear at dozens of independent clothiers that specialize in high-end fashion or more adventurous apparel with an edge. Several designers such as Luly Yang and Karan Dannenberg have their own shops in Belltown (see p68) and Fremont (see p86), and many upscale boutiques dot the 5th Avenue area south of Pike Street.

3 Malls

As with most United States cities, large malls need the expansive and cheaper real estate found only in suburbs or outlying areas. However, there are smaller, somewhat pricey urban malls including Westlake Mall, Pacific Place, and Rainier Square (see pp52–3). They also

include familiar chain stores as well as locally owned ventures.

4 Flea Markets & Thrift Shops

If you like secondhand merchandise, you'll find bargains all over town. Many neighborhoods, including Ballard and Fremont, have outdoor farmers' markets on Sundays. There are also plenty of thrift shops; the best of these are Salvation Army, Value Village, and Seattle Goodwill, located on Capitol Hill and the ID. ✪ Salvation Army: Map E6; 1000 4th Ave S • Value Village: Map M3; 1525 11th Ave • Seattle Goodwill: Map F6; 1400 S Lane St

5 Garage & Sidewalk Sales

Walk or drive through any neighborhood on weekend mornings and you'll find a treasure trove of clothing, toys, furniture, and electronics up for sale. Look for large signs on telephone polls, or scour the newspaper classified ads to find appropriate listings.

6 Bargaining

Most consumers in the US are uncomfortable with bargaining tactics, and bargaining is never acceptable at chains or in department stores. However, at flea markets and yard sales, it is common to negotiate for a better price.

7 Sales Tax

With the exception of groceries, all Seattle retail purchases are subject to combined state and city sales taxes of 9.5 percent.

8 Convenience Stores

It's relatively common to find a convenience store in commercial areas, even in exclusive neighborhoods. They sell a little bit of everything from fresh produce to deli items, snack food and drink, toiletries, and general supply merchandise. Remember you would pay considerably more than in supermarkets or drugstores.

9 Refunds

Always find out a store's policy on exchanging or returning items, or on obtaining credit. National chain stores often have a liberal return policy that may enable you to return goods at another branch once you're back at home.

10 Washington Attorney General's Office Consumer Protection Division

If a retailer or service provider has dealt with you in an illegal fashion, take your complaint here so that court proceedings can be initiated or sanctions be employed against the perpetrator. ✪ 1-800-551-4636; www.atg.wa.gov

For any unresolved complaints on a product you have purchased, call the Better Business Bureau at (206) 431-2222.

Left **Sushi** Center **Red wine** Right **Beer bottle labels**

TOP 10 Eating & Accommodation Tips

1 Pacific Rim Cuisine
In Seattle, this cuisine refers to fresh Pacific Northwest ingredients combined with the flavors and cooking techniques of countries bordering the Pacific Ocean. Chefs create masterpieces and signature dishes using sushi-grade fish, Kobe-style beef, ginger- and soy-based sauces, and handmade noodles to complement US menu mainstays.

2 Other Cuisines
You can hardly walk a block without meeting up with a Thai restaurant. Mexican taquerias compete with establishments serving Spanish tapas, while French and Italian bistros still attract crowds. Indian restaurants often include Pakistani, Tibetan, and Nepalese dishes as well.

3 Reservations
It's advisable to secure lunch or dinner reservations at formal or expensive restaurants, or at those with a view. Alternatively, consider dining at a non-peak hour, as getting a table anywhere special at noon or 6pm is a challenge.

4 Drinks
Washington has its share of award-winning vineyards. Better restaurants employ *sommeliers* to assist you in choosing wines to complement your meal, and they can also steer you toward a selection based on price. If beer or ale suits your taste, Washington has many microbreweries emulating the heavier British styles of ales and stouts, as well as crisp German lagers and Belgian Abbey ales.

5 Tax & Tipping
Restaurants add 10 percent sales tax to the total bill, and it's customary to leave a tip of at least 15 percent (see p107).

6 Choosing Hotel Locations
For an urban experience or a central location, downtown is the hands-down pick. If you have a car or don't mind the distance, a number of B&Bs, boutique hotels, or guesthouses (see pp114–19) border the downtown area.

7 Hotel Gradings
All major hotels are subject to two widely accepted diamond- or star-based systems that gauge the overall merits, level of service, and amenities advertised by the property. Four-star/five-diamond hotels are the most luxurious and expensive. If you are unsure, ask the reservation agent if the hotel has a rating. Hotels rarely mention status unless they have a high score.

8 Making Hotel Reservations
Seattle has become a worldwide destination for huge conventions and large tour groups, many coming from cruise ships in the summer months when the tourist industry flourishes. Make your reservations in advance to avoid finding only a limited choice on arrival.

9 Extra Costs & Tipping
Occasionally, travel packages at downtown hotels include overnight parking with the room, but most charge exorbitant rates for the service. You are charged for making phones calls even when dialing a toll-free number. If the room includes a stocked refrigerator, anything consumed will add to the bill. Also remember to tip the housekeeper and other service providers at the hotel.

10 Traveling with Kids
Many hotels don't charge extra for kids 12 and under staying in their parents' room. Some have the same service for children 18 and under. Others may provide roll-away beds or cribs for a price. Search the neighborhood around Seattle Center for the most family-friendly hotels or motels. Parking lots nearby are often cheaper than the hotel's garage.

Left **Fairmont Olympic Hotel** Right **The Edgewater Hotel meeting room**

TOP 10 Traditional Hotels

1 The Westin Seattle Hotel

Located in two round towers, the Westin has an indoor pool, 24-hour room service, in-room movies, valet/laundry, a restaurant and lobby bar, a business center, and non-smoking rooms. ⊛ *Map K3 • 1900 5th Ave • (206) 728-1000 • www. westinseattle.com • $$$$*

2 Fairmont Olympic Hotel

One of the Pacific Northwest's most lauded properties, this landmark hotel has treated guests with the utmost elegance and personalized service since it opened in 1924. ⊛ *Map K4 • 411 University St • 1-888-363-5022 • www.fairmont.com • $$$$$*

3 Hilton Seattle

Its proximity to the Convention Center makes the Hilton popular with business travelers. All rooms are above the 14th floor, affording phenomenal views. Free web TV, as well as such amenities as mini-bars, coffee-makers, and hair-dryers, are provided. Check out their senior citizen and family discount plans. ⊛ *Map K4 • 1301 6th Ave • 1-800-426-0535 • www.thehilton seattle.com • $$$*

4 Sheraton Seattle

Guests can relax in front of the cozy lobby fireplace or head for

The Daily Grill Bar for delicious hot and cold *hors d'oeuvres*, Washington state's award-winning wines, martinis, and plasma TVs for sports and news. ⊛ *Map K4 • 1400 6th Ave • (206) 621-9000 • www.sheraton.com/seattle • $$$*

5 Grand Hyatt Seattle

This elegant hotel's deluxe rooms feature cordless, two-line phones and Internet access. Guests have free use of the sprawling health club, which has an exercise room, sauna, Jacuzzi, steam bath, lockers, circuit machines, and cardio machines with flat-screen televisions. ⊛ *Map K3 • 721 Pine St • (206) 774-1234 • www.grandseattle.hyatt.com • $$$$*

6 Renaissance Seattle

This deluxe hotel has a penthouse swimming pool, a whirlpool tub, and a workout room. It is near many major attractions. ⊛ *Map K5 • 515 Madison St • (206) 583-0300 • www.marriott.com • $$$$*

7 Seattle Marriott Waterfront

This waterfront gem with excellent views of Puget Sound and the Olympic Mountains is Seattle's first full-service hotel. There's a fitness center and two restaurants.

⊛ *Map H4 • 2100 Alaskan Way • (206) 443-5000 • www.marriott.com • $$$$$*

8 The Edgewater Hotel

All rooms combine luxury with Pacific Northwest charm. Features include handcrafted pine furniture, river rock fireplaces, Ralph Lauren bedding, turn-down service, deluxe bath amenities, and in-room Starbucks coffee service. A perfect alternative to downtown hotels. ⊛ *Map H4 • 2411 Alaskan Way, Pier 67 • 1-800-624-0670 • www.edgewaterhotel.com • $$$$*

9 Courtyard Seattle Downtown/ Lake Union

One of Marriott's less expensive hotels, offers great lake views and proximity to Seattle Center and I-5. Rooms have free Internet access, and there's an indoor pool and fitness center. ⊛ *Map J1 • 925 Westlake Ave N • (206) 213-0100 • www.marriott.com • $$*

10 Crowne Plaza Hotel Seattle

A reputable chain hotel with well-appointed rooms and trendy boutiques. Guests can avail of the 24-hour fitness center and business center. An easy walk to the Convention Center. ⊛ *Map K4 • 1113 6th Ave • (206) 464-1980 • www.cphotelseattle.com • $$*

Unless otherwise stated, all traditional hotels accept credit cards, and have disabled access, en-suite bathrooms, and air conditioning.

Price Categories

For a standard, double room per night (with breakfast if included), taxes and extra charges.

$	under $100
$$	$100–200
$$$	$200–250
$$$$	$250–300
$$$$$	over $300

Alexis Hotel

TOP 10 Boutique Hotels

1 W Seattle

This sleek property attracts the hip, trendy, and well-heeled. It offers modern amenities, impeccable service, and signature ultra-comfortable beds. ◎ Map K4 • 1112 4th Ave • (206) 264-6000 • www.wseattle.com • Dis. access • $$$$$

2 Hotel Monaco

What was once a phone company's switching center is now a sophisticated hotel. All rooms come with flat-screen TVs. ◎ Map K4 • 1101 4th Ave • (206) 621-1770 • www.monaco-seattle.com • Dis. access • $$$$

3 Mayflower Park Hotel

Built in 1927, this is one of Seattle's last independently owned hotels. Room designs reflect common Queen Anne touches in subtle and dark hues. The house restaurant is Andaluca, a small, top-rated establishment with excellent Mediterranean fare. The adjoining bar, Oliver's, makes exquisite martinis. ◎ Map J4 • 405 Olive Way • 1-800-426-5100 • www.mayflowerpark.com • Dis. access • $$$$

4 Sorrento Hotel

At the opulent Sorrento guests find Seattle's finest luxury boutique hotel as well as a destination gourmet restaurant, the Hunt Club. Take pleasure in Italian marble bathrooms, 400-thread-count Egyptian cotton linens, and a complimentary car service within downtown. ◎ Map L4 • 900 Madison St • 1-800-426-1265 • www.hotelsorrento.com • Dis. access • $$$$

5 Alexis Hotel

Since 1901, the Alexis has lived up to its stellar reputation as an elegant haven for those who prefer pampering. Evening wine tasting, 24-hour room service, Internet access, steam and fitness room, full day spa, and the Bookstore Bar are some of the highlights. ◎ Map K5 • 1007 1st Ave • 1-866-356-8894 • www.alexishotel.com • Dis. access • $$$$$

6 Hotel Vintage Seattle

Part of the upscale Kimpton group, this hotel offers such comforts as plush terrycloth robes, lush fabrics and cherry wood furniture, and a hosted wine hour by a wood-burning fireplace in the lobby. Try Tulio, the award-winning Italian restaurant downstairs for a sumptuous dinner. ◎ Map K4 • 1100 5th Ave • 1-800-853-3914 • www.hotelvintage-seattle.com • Dis. access • $$$$

7 The Roosevelt Hotel

This 1929-era hotel named for the 26th United States president is centrally located, near downtown's best shopping. Evenings bring live jazz piano to the lobby, where visitors gather to relax. ◎ Map K4 • 1531 7th Ave • 1-800-663-1144 • www.coasthotels.com • Dis. access • $$$

8 Hotel Max

Formerly the Vance, this hip boutique hotel features original artwork by local artists. Located in the heart of downtown. ◎ Map K3 • 620 Stewart St • (206) 728-6299 • www.hotelmaxseattle.com • Dis. access • $$

9 Inn at Virginia Mason

Owned by the nearby Virginia Mason Hospital (see p111), this 1920s-era inn entices visitors with wood-burning fireplaces in some rooms, a rooftop café, and excellent city views from residential First Hill. ◎ Map L4 • 1006 Spring St • 1-800-283-6453 • www.innatvirginiamason.com • Dis. access • $$

10 Hotel Ändra

This sophisticated, remodeled hotel in downtown Seattle offers top-notch service and a boutique experience to its guests. Scandinavian design elements can be seen in all of the 119 rooms and luxury suites. ◎ Map J3 • 2000 4th Ave • (206) 448-8600 • www.hotelandra.com • Dis. access • $$$$

Left **University Inn outdoor pool** Right **Watertown**

TOP 10 Neighborhood Hotels

1 Ace Hotel

This hotel, situated in a historic building in the heart of Belltown, appeals to guests who prefer location over luxury. There are few amenities; instead the emphasis is on ultra-modern decor. Pike Place Market and Capitol Hill are nearby. ⊕ *Map H3 • 2423 1st Ave • (206) 448-4721 • www.acehotel.com • $$$*

2 MarQueen Hotel

Queen Anne neighborhood's stately hotel provides a wonderful alternative to the area's chain motels and hotels. Walk to quaint cafés, trendy bars, and small shops. Double-glazed windows have all but eliminated the din from foot traffic heading to or from concerts and sports events. ⊕ *Map G1 • 600 Queen Anne Ave N • (206) 282-7407 • www.marqueen.com • Dis. access • $$$*

3 University Inn

Parents and students reserve early to save their spot at the University Inn, a non-smoking property located only three blocks from the University of Washington. Guests are treated to a free Continental breakfast and a courtesy shuttle to downtown. ⊕ *Map E2 • 4140 Roosevelt Way NE • (206) 632-5055 • www.universityinnseattle.com • Dis. access • $$*

4 Best Western Plus Pioneer Square

History buffs and sports fans flock to this 19th-century landmark hotel featuring period decor and deluxe bathrooms. The bustling waterfront, ferry terminal, stadiums, and Pioneer Square historic district lie just outside. ⊕ *Map K5 • 77 Yesler Way • 1-800-800-5514 • www.pioneer square.com • Dis. access • $$*

5 Inn at the Market

This inn pampers guests in an enviable locale with panoramic views of the Olympic Range and Mount Rainier. Consider dining at Campagne, the classic French restaurant, or its more casual country-style café. ⊕ *Map J4 • 86 Pine St • 1-800-446-4484 • www.innatthemarket.com • Dis. access • $$$*

6 Inn at Queen Anne

Charm and a cozy ambience characterize this 1930s-era inn. Rooms have kitchenettes and there's a plant-filled patio/courtyard on the property, perfect for sipping tea or coffee. ⊕ *Map G2 • 505 1st Ave N • 1-800-952-5043 • www.innatqueenanne.com • $$*

7 Silver Cloud Inn

This affordable Lake Union neighborhood inn provides complimentary breakfasts and shuttles to downtown. Many rooms have views of Lake Union and its sea-plane traffic. ⊕ *Map K1 • 1150 Fairview Ave N • 1-800-330-5812 • www.silvercloud.com • Dis. access • $$$*

8 Hotel 1000

An upscale hotel in a great downtown location. Rooms feature fine Thai linens, two-person tubs, and state-of-the-art entertainment centers. ⊕ *Map K4 • 1000 1st Ave • (206) 957-1000 • www.hotel1000seattle.com • Dis. access • $$$*

9 Hotel Deca

An attractive choice for visiting parents, professors, and students, this award-winning hotel has 16 stories and designer rooms that offer comfy digs and great views of the U-District, the Space Needle, and the downtown skyline. ⊕ *Map E2 • 4507 Brooklyn Ave NE • 1-800-899-0251 • www.hoteldeca.com • Dis. access • $$$*

10 Watertown

Essentially a hotel catering to students and their parents, Watertown boasts non-smoking premises, free parking, loaner bicycles, and a free shuttle to select attractions. ⊕ *Map E2 • 4242 Roosevelt Way NE • (206) 826-4242 • www.watertownseattle.com • Dis. access • $$*

Be sure to check your hotel's cancellation policy. Some require 14 days' advance notice if you change your mind.

Price Categories

For a standard, double room per night (with breakfast if included), taxes and extra charges.	$ under $100
	$$ $100–200
	$$$ $200–250
	$$$$ $250–300
	$$$$$ over $300

Pensione Nichols

TOP 10 B&Bs & Guesthouses

1 Pensione Nichols

Personalized services and its proximity to downtown make Pensione Nichols B&B a decent in-city choice. It may be a little worn on the edges, but the clear views of sparkling Puget Sound are great. • Map J4 • 1923 1st Ave • (206) 441-7125 • www.pensione nichols.com • No air conditioning • $$

2 Gaslight Inn

This lovingly restored 19th-century inn inspires guests with its notable private art collection. Highlights include a heated outdoor pool, fireplaces, and stunning views. • Map E4 • 1727 15th Ave • (206) 325-3654 • www.gaslight-inn. com • Some rooms have shared bath • No air conditioning • $$

3 Bed & Breakfast on Broadway

Located in a historical residential neighborhood north of the popular entertainment district, the features here include a parlor with grand piano, fireplace, Oriental rugs, antiques, and polished hardwood floors. • Map L1 • 722 Broadway E • (206) 329-8933 • www.bbonbroadway.com • No air conditioning • $$

4 11th Avenue Inn

This quiet neighborhood bed and breakfast is housed in a charming 1906 Victorian inn. The eight guestrooms are decorated with antique furnishings and boast modern amenities including wireless Internet access. All have queen beds and private bathrooms. Free on-site parking and within walking distance of downtown. • Map M3 • 121 11th Ave E • 1-800-720-7161 • www. 11thavenueinn.com • No air conditioning • $$

5 Bacon Mansion Bed & Breakfast

This 1909 Edwardian Tudor mansion exudes elegance with original carved wood trim, 3,000-crystal chandelier, marble fireplaces, and a remarkable library. Most rooms have private baths. • Map E4 • 959 Broadway E • 1-800-240-1864 • www.bacon mansion.com • Dis. access • No air conditioning • $$

6 Shafer Baillie Mansion

This Tudor Revival mansion has clean, well-appointed en-suite rooms that include free Wi-Fi. Located within walking distance of Volunteer Park and the Seattle Asian Art Museum. • Map E4 • 907 14th Ave E • (206) 322-4654 • www.sbmansion.com • $$

7 Greenlake Guest House

This 1920s Craftsman house is located on Green Lake Park, a popular recreational hub in North Seattle. There are four guest rooms with private bath. The house enjoys good views over the lake. Special romance packages are available. • Map D1 • 7630 E Green Lake Dr. N • (206) 729-8700 • www.greenlake guesthouse.com • $$

8 Hill House B&B

Sofas covered in silk or tapestries, beveled windows draped with chintz swags, hardwood floors, and lovely Persian rugs grace these nine Victorian houses. • Map M2 • 1113 East John St • 1-866-417-4455 • www. seattlehillhouse.com • No air conditioning • $$

9 Mildred's B&B

This large, double-turreted 1890 Victorian inn takes guests back in time with lace curtains, red carpets, and a wraparound front porch that's perfect for lounging. • Map E4 • 1202 15th Ave E • 1-800-327-9692 • www. mildredsbnb.com • No air conditioning • $$

10 Swallow's Nest Guest Cottages

A 15-minute ferry ride from West Seattle to Vashon Island (see p56) brings you to this hideaway of eight charming cottages, some in woodland, others with views of Mount Rainier and the island's quaint harbor. • Map N3 • 6030 248th St SW, Vashon/Maury Island • 1-800-269-6378 • www. vashonislandcottages.com • $$

Rooms in older homes and guesthouses may not have en-suite bathrooms or air conditioning.

Left **Travelodge Seattle Center** Right **Green Tortoise Hostel**

Budget Hotels & Hostels

1 Kings Inn
The inn includes free parking with your nightly rate, and local and toll-free calls are gratis. Suites come with coffee-maker, microwave, and a refrigerator. There's also a coin-op laundry on the premises. ◎ *Map J3 • 2106 5th Ave • (206) 441-8833 • www.kingsinn seattle.com • $$*

2 Travelodge Seattle Center
Comfortable rooms, in-room coffee, and free local calls at this motel near the Space Needle. Amenities are few, but there is a children's play area, free Continental breakfast, an outdoor pool, and parking for guests. ◎ *Map J2 • 200 6th Ave N • (206) 441-7878 • www.travelodge.com • Dis. access • $$*

3 Extended Stay America - Seattle - Bellevue - Downtown
This wallet-friendly hotel is best for longer stays – Each studio contains a fully-equipped kitchen, with a refrigerator, micro-wave and coffee-maker. Also, free Wi-Fi and breakfast. ◎ *Map P2 • 11400 Main St • (425) 453-8186 • www.extendedstayamerica. com • Dis. access • $$*

4 Moore Hotel
Simple, comfortable rooms, some with shared bathroom, in a great location two blocks from Pikes Peak Market. Free Wi-Fi. ◎ *Map J4 • 1926 2nd Ave • 1-800-421-5508 • www.moorehotel.com • No air conditioning • $$*

5 Warwick Seattle Hotel
This hotel is a first-rate choice for travelers who want basic amenities at much lower prices. On top of many 24-hour extras such as room service, business and fitness center, and courtesy van for anywhere within 2 miles (3 km), there's also Internet access, and rooms trimmed in fine woods and marble. ◎ *Map J3 • 401 Lenora St • (206) 443-4300 • www.warwick wa.com • Dis. access • $$*

6 University Motel Suites
This budget option is just a few blocks from the I-5, so downtown is only a quick drive away. Small suites have a living/kitchen area, a bedroom, and a full bath. Free HBO, Wi-Fi, and parking, plus on-site laundry facilities. ◎ *Map E2 • 4731 12th Ave NE • (206) 522-4724 • www.university motelsuites.com • $$*

7 The Maxwell Hotel Seattle
A locally owned hotel at the base of Queen Anne Hill, adjacent to the Space Needle, with spacious rooms. Facilities include an indoor pool, free bicycle use, and free parking ◎ *Map H1 • 300 Roy St • (866) 866-7977 • www. themaxwellhotel.com • $$*

8 Panama Hotel
Sabro Ozasa, a Japanese architect and graduate of the University of Washington, built this hotel in 1910. Since then, it has housed Japanese immigrants, Alaskan fisherman, and international travelers. Rooms have sinks only, but shared bathrooms have clawfoot tubs. A multilingual staff is on hand to assist guests. Free Wi-Fi. ◎ *Map L6 • 605 S Main St • (206) 223-9242 • www.panama hotelseattle.com • No air conditioning • $$*

9 Green Tortoise Hostel
Backpackers, students, and US travelers on the cheap frequent this hostel as its rates include free breakfast, Internet access, and retail discount card. ◎ *Map J4 • 105 Pike St • (206) 340-1222 • www.greentortoise. net • No air conditioning • $*

10 City Hostel Seattle
Award-winning budget accommodations set this hostel above the rest, and it's just a short walk from most tourist attractions. Local artists display their work on the walls, and movie-makers show films in the small theater. The price includes breakfast, Wi-Fi, a library, and three kitchens. ◎ *Map H3 • 2327 2nd Ave • (206) 706-3255 • www.hostelseattle. com • Dis. access • $*

Find the best deals by calling the hotel's main reservation number.

Price Categories

For a standard,	
double room per	$ under $100
night (with breakfast	$$ $100–200
if included), taxes	$$$ $200–250
and extra charges.	$$$$ $250–300
	$$$$$ over $300

Chambered Nautilus Bed & Breakfast Inn

🔟 Apartments & Private Homes

1 Accommodations Plus Inc.
Corporate clients as well as leisure travelers take advantage of this outfit's decent rates for fully furnished and comfortable rooms. Most Puget Sound-area apartments have fully equipped kitchens, linens, all utilities and biweekly maid service. ✆ 1-800-583-1613 • www.aplusnw.com • $$

2 Belltown Inn
Located in the heart of hip Belltown, this complex features fully furnished studios with kitchenettes. A short walk from Pike Place Market and on the free Metro bus line, it's an affordable week- or month-long option. ✆ Map J3 • 2301 3rd Ave • (206) 529-3700 • www. belltown-inn.com • $$

3 Chelsea Station Inn
The Chelsea Station Inn offers four large suites and access to 24-hour snacks. Situated at the south entrance of Woodland Park Zoo and a short walk to Green Lake. ✆ Map D2 • 4915 Linden Ave N • (206) 547-6077 • www.chelseastationinn. com • Dis. access • $$$

4 Sea to Sky Rentals
This property management company represents over 30 apartments, condos, and homes throughout Seattle. Amenities include Internet access, parking, and the flexibility of daily, weekly, or monthly rates. ✆ Map C2 • 118 N 36th St • (206) 632-4210 • www.seatosky rentals.com • $$

5 Seattle Suites
Booking an affordable executive suite downtown provides an upscale alternative for families or individuals looking for unique accommodations. Each apartment is fully furnished, and many offer fabulous city views. Enjoy complimentary Starbucks coffee and a games room with a pool table and big-screen TV. Weekly and monthly rates are available; minimum stays of three nights. ✆ Map K4 • 1400 Hubbell Place #1103 • (206) 232-2799 • www. seattlesuite.com • $$

6 Chambered Nautilus Bed & Breakfast Inn
This gracious 1915 Georgian Colonial home is close to the University of Washington campus. Four rooms have porches overlooking gardens and mountains, and guests stay in nicely furnished one- or two-bedroom apartments. ✆ Map F2 • 5005 22nd Ave NE • 1-800-545-8459 • www. chamberednautilus.com • $$

7 First Hill Apartments
A good, economical choice just blocks from downtown, this secure complex of apartments offers everything from tiny studios to luxury loft suites, all fully furnished and well equipped. There is also free garage parking available. ✆ Map M5 • 400 10th Ave • (206) 621-9229 • www.firsthillapts. com • Dis. access • $$

8 The Mediterranean Inn
Non-smoking, furnished studio apartments near the Seattle Center in the lower Queen Anne neighborhood. Each unit has a kitchenette. Parking is available for a fee, and there is also an exercise room. Walking distance to downtown. ✆ Map G1 • 425 Queen Anne Ave N • (866) 525-4700 • www. mediterranean-inn.com • $$

9 Short-Term Suites
Choose from a range of fully furnished corporate suites located in many favored Seattle neighborhoods, such as Queen Anne, Fremont, Capitol Hill, and First Hill. These accommodations are priced to fit every need and budget. Minimum month-long stay. ✆ (206) 276-0588 • www. shorttermsuites.com • $$

10 Home Exchange Inc.
As a member of the Home Exchange club, you can arrange to trade homes with a Seattleite at a time that is convenient to both parties. ✆ 1-800-877-8723 • www. homeexchange.com

Unless otherwise stated, all hotels accept credit cards, and have en-suite bathrooms and air conditioning.

General Index

1962 World's Fair 6, 11, 32
5th Avenue Boutiques 52
5th Avenue Theatre 38
11th Avenue Inn 117

A

Accommodations Plus Inc. 119
Ace Hotel 116
ACT Theatre/ Kreielsheimer Place 39
Adobe Systems 84
Agua Verde Café & Paddle Club 22, 45
Alaska Gold Rush 30, 52
Alaska-Yukon-Pacific Exposition 22
Alexis Hotel 115
Alki Beach 96, 99
Alki Beach Park 99
Alki Point 30, 97
All Together Skatepark 86
Allen, Paul 10, 31, 72
AllSaints 69
Anderson, Guy 37
Ann Starrett Mansion 57
Annapurna Café 77
Anthony's HomePort 93
Anthony's Pier 66 & Bell St Diner 12
Aoki 77
Arboretum 20, 47
architecture **32–33**
Area 51, 73
Art Institute of Seattle 66
Assaggio Ristorante 65, 67
Austin A. Bell Building 66
Avalon Glass Works 100
Azuma 51
Azuma Sushi 101

B

Babeland 73, 74
Baby & Co. 68
Backdoor at Roxy's, The 85
Bacon Mansion Bed & Breakfast 117
Badanes, Steve 82
Bagley Wright Theatre 11, 38
   Seattle Repertory Group 11
   Seattle Repertory Theatre 38

Bainbridge Island 12, 56
Bakery Nouveau 101
Ballard 20, 21, **88–93**
   Ballard Avenue 90
   Bardahl Sign 91
   map 88
   Market Street 89
   places to eat 93
   shops 92
   Sunday Farmers Market 90
Ballard Inn 91
banking & communications **110**
Bauer, Eddie 31, 69
Bauhaus Books & Coffee 43, 73, 75
Bed & Breakfast on Broadway 117
Bella Umbrella 69
Belle Fleur 86
Bellevue 54
   Old Bellevue 54
Belltown 48, 65, 66, 68
   Around Belltown 66
   places to eat 67
   shops 68
Belltown Billiards 66
Belltown Inn 119
Belltown Pizza 67
Belvedere Park 98
Benaroya Hall 38, 51
   Seattle Symphony 38
Best Western Plus Pioneer Square 116
Beyer, Richard 81
Bezos, Jeff 31
Big Four Mountain 59
   Big Four Ice Caves 59
Big Time Brewery & Alehouse 22, 49
Bill Speidel's Underground Tour 14, 33
Blue C Sushi 87
boating 21
Boeing 30
   Boeing, William E. 30
Bon Marche 53
Borofsky, Jonathan 36
Brad's Swingside Café 87
BrasilFest 35
Broadway 7, **18–19**, 71
   Dance Steps on Broadway 18
Broadway Performance Hall 18, 39

Brooklyn Seafood, Steak & Oyster House, The 51
Brothers, Olmsted 46, 57, 72
Buck, Peter 48
budget tips **108**
Bumbershoot 11, 34
Bundy, Ted 31
Burke, Judge Thomas 44
Burke-Gilman Trail 44, 82, 84
   bridges 84
   dock overlook 84
   gravel plant 84
   old trolley barn 84
   rope swing 84
Burke Museum 23, 36
buses 105
Bushell's Auction 53

C

Café Allegro 43
Café Besalu 43
Café Campagne 8
Café Juanita 51
cafés 43
Caffé Ladro 43
Caffé Vita 75
Cal Anderson Park 18
Calder, Alexander 13
Callahan, Kenneth 37
Camelion Design 92
Camlin 41, 115
Camp Long 98
Canlis 50
Capitol Hill 7, 18, 23, 48, **70–77**
   cafés & taverns 75
   cathedrals 71
   gay/lesbian scene 71
   map 70
   neighborhood homes 73
   Pike/Pine Corridor 71
   Pill Hill 19
   places to eat 76
   shops 76
Card Kingdom 92
Carl S. English, Jr. Botanical Gardens 89
Carmilia's 100
Carpenter, Lewis 82
Cascades 44
Cassatt, Mary 36
Center for Urban Horticulture 47

Center for Wooden Boats
21, 37, 45
Central Library 32, 64
CenturyLink Field 16
Chambered Nautilus
Bed & Breakfast Inn 119
Chateau Ste. Michelle 54
Chelan Café 101
Chelsea Station 119
Chihuly, Dale 37
Chihuly Bridge 56
children's attractions
40–41
Children's Film Festival
Seattle 40
Children's Museum 40
Chiso 51
Chittenden, Hiram M. 20
Chongqing 47
Chop Suey 48, 75
cinemas 39
Cinerama 39
City Hostel Seattle 118
Clementine 100
Coast Guard Station 99
Colman Pool 44, 47
Columbia Center 32, 64
Comet Tavern 73, 75
Constellation Beach 97
consulates 111
courier services 110
Courtyard Seattle Down-
town/Lake Union 114
credit cards 110
Crescent Lounge, The 74
Crest 54
Crossroads Shopping
Center 55
Crowne Plaza Hotel
Seattle 114
Crypt Off Broadway 76
Curious Kidstuff 100
Cuff Complex, The 74
Cyclops 67

D
Dahlia Lounge 51, 67
Dandelion Botanical
Company 91, 92
Day Trips: Islands &
Historic Towns **56–57**
Day Trips: Mountain
Getaways **58–59**
Daybreak Star Indian
Cultural Center 26, 34
DeLaurenti 9
DeLille Cellars 54
DeLuxe Bar & Grill 77

Denny, Arthur A. 6, 30, 64, 97
Denny Party 30
Denny Creek 58
Denny Hill 64
Denny Regrade 64
Día de Muertos 35
Dick's Drive-In 19
Dimitriou's Jazz Alley 48
Dinosaur Topiaries 82
Discovery Park 7, **26–27**
West Point Treatment
Plant 27
Dock Street Brokers 91
Don Armeni Park 99
Donier, Kaspar 50
Douglas, Tom 51
Downtown **62–69**
map 61
shops 69
Downtown Seattle Transit
Tunnel 33
Drug Plant Garden 23
Dusty Strings 86
Duwamish River 97
Duxiana 65

E
Eagle 74
Eagles Auditorium 39
Eakins, Thomas 36
Earshot Jazz Festival 35
Eastlake 73
Eastside **54–55**
floating bridges 54
Easy Street Records 100
eating & accommodation
tips **113**
Edge of the Circle Books 76
Edgewater Hotel, The 114
Edie's Shoes 76
Egyptian Theatre 19, 39,
70, 73
El Camino 87
El Corazón 49
El Gaucho 67
Elliott Bay Brewing
Company 49
Elliott Bay 26, 64, 98
Elliott Bay Book Company
& Café 43, 73, 76
readings & lectures 43
Elysian Brewing Company
49, 73, 75
embassies 104
emergencies 111
EMP Museum 6, 10, 32,
39, 72, 108
Endless Knot 68

Esquin Wine Merchants
68
Essenza 86
ETG 83
evo 86
Exact 97, 98
Extended Stay America
- Seattle - Bellevue -
Downtown 118

F
Facelli Winery 54
Fairmont Olympic Hotel
41, 114
famous Seattleites 31
Fauntleroy Ferry Terminal
47, 56, 97
Feathered Friends 45
Festa Italiana 35
Festál cultural events 35
Festival Sundiata 35
festivals & parades **34–35**
Fire Bell Tower 57
First and Pike News 9
First Hill 19
First Hill Apartments 119
Fisher, Elmer H. 33
Fishermen's Terminal 90
Folger, Captain 98
Fort Worden State Park 57
Fox's Gem Shop 65
Frame Up Studios 86
Freedom Day March 34, 71
Freeway Park 62
Fremont 20, 42, **80–87**
culture 85
First Fridays Art Walk 85
Fremont library 85
glass art 85
map 80
places to eat 87
pumpkin-carving
contests 85
shops 86
Fremont Arts Council 82,
85
Fremont Bridge 81, 83
Fremont Coffee Company
43
Fremont Fair 85
Fremont Fair Solstice
Parade 34
Fremont Ferry & Sunday
Ice Cream Cruise 82
Fremont Outdoor Cinema
39, 83
Fremont Troll 82
Fremont Vintage Mall 86

Friday Harbor 56
Frisell, Bill 35
Frye Art Museum 36

G
Gallery 1412 49
Garage 77
Gas Works Park 42, 44, 46
Gaslight Inn 117
Gates, Bill 31, 54
Gates Estate 54
gay, lesbian, bisexual, & transgender venues **74**
gays & lesbians 34, 109
Gehry, Frank 10, 32, 72
getting around Seattle **106**
  boat 106
  buses 106
  commuter rail 106
  ferries 106
  seaplane 106
getting physical **44–45**
  scuba diving 45
  windsurfing 45
Gilman, Daniel 44
Golden Gardens 21, 45, 47, 88, 90
Grand Central Bakery 15
Grand Hyatt Seattle 114
Grand Illusion 39
Graves, Morris 37
Great Fire of 1889 14, 30, 91
Great Northern Railway 30
Great Wall Mall 17
Green River Killer 31
Green Tortoise Hostel 118
Green Lake 42, 46
Greenlake Boat Rentals 45
Greenlake Guest House 117
Gregg's Greenlake Cycles 45

H
Hale's Ales Brewery 49, 87
Hana 51
Hanks, Tom 21
Harbor City Restaurant 16
Harbor Island 97
Harbor Steps 62
Harem Off Broadway 76
Harvard Exit 19, 39, 70
Hattie's Hat 93
helplines 111
Hendrix, Jimi 31
Hendrix Statue 72
Henry Art Gallery 22, 36

Herbfarm, The 50
Herkimer Coffee 43
Highland Ice Arena 44
Hill House B&B 117
Hilton Seattle 114
Hiram M. Chittenden Locks 21, 81, 89
historic preservation 43
history **30–31**
History House 81
Hmong Flower Stalls 9
Hmong New Year 35
Home Exchange Inc. 119
HoneyHole 77
Hopvine Pub 75
Horiuchi, Paul 37
Horseshoe 91, 92
hospitals & clinics 111
Hotel 1000 116
Hotel Ändra 115
Hotel Deca 116
Hotel Max 115
Hotel Monaco 115
Hotel Vintage Seattle 115
hotels 41, **114–119**
Hsu, Joe 17
Hub and Bespoke 86
Hugo, Richard 72
Husky Stadium 20, 23
  UW Huskies 23
Hyatt Place Seattle Downtown 41

I
I Love Sushi 51
Iida, Juki 47
Il Bistro 8
IIndia Bistro 93
Indoor Sun Shoppe 84
Inn at Queen Anne 116
Inn at the Market 116
Inn at Virginia Mason 115
International District 6, 12, **16–17**, 33
  Chinatown 16
  Chinese Lunar New Year 16
  dim sum 17
International Fountain 40
Irish Week Festival 35
Isadoras Antique Jewelry 69
Issaquah Alps 58

J
Jade Garden 16
Jak's Grill 101
James, Clayton 37

Japanese Garden 47
Jeffrey Moose Gallery 65
Jewel Box Theater 66
JF Henry Cooking & Dining 100
John Fluevog Shoes 69

K
Kane Hall 22
Karan Dannenberg Clothier 68
Kavu 91
Kelly, Ellsworth 13
Kenmore Air 105
KEPX 104
KeyArena 11, 38
Kezner, Larry 82
kids' bookstores & galleries 40
Kings Inn 118
Kirkland 54
Klondike Gold Rush 30
Klondike Gold Rush National Historical Park 15
Koolhaas, Rem 32
Kozue 51
KuKuRuZa Gourmet Popcorn 92
KUOW 104
Kwanjai 87

L
La Carta de Oaxaca 93
La Rustica 101
Lake Cushman 59
Lake Union 21, 44
Lake View Cemetery 72
Lake Washington 34, 45, 54
Lake Washington Rowing Club 84
Lake Washington Ship Canal 7, **20–21**, 80, 81, 83
  bascule bridges 20
  boating 21
  Christmas ships 21
  making the cut 20
  working waterfront 21
Lambert House Gay Youth Center 74
Lark 50, 77
Lawrence, Jacob 37
Le Frock 73
Leavenworth 57
Leavenworth Nutcracker Museum 57
Lee, Bruce 31, 48, 72

Lenin Statue 82
Lenora Street Bridge 66
Les Amis 86
Lesbian Resource Center 74
Lighthouse Roasters 43
Lincoln Park 44, 47, 97
Linda's Tavern 73, 75
Local 360 67
Little Saigon 16
Locke, Gary 31
Lockspot Café 93
Log House Museum 98
LUCCA Great Finds 92
Lumber Mills 30
Luna Park Café 101
Luther Burbank Park 55

M
Mac & Jack's 49
Mackie, Jack 18
Macrina Bakery 67
Macy's 53, 112
Made in Washington 65
Magic Mouse Toys 40
Majestic Bay 39
Mama's Mexican Kitchen 67
Maneki 51
Mariners Team Store 69
Maritime Pacific Brewing Company 49
Market Street 91
MarQueen Hotel 116
Marriott Courtyard 41
Martin-Zambito Gallery 76
Marymoor Park 55
Maxwell Hotel Seattle, The 41, 118
Mayflower Park Hotel 115
McCaw Hall 10, 38
   Pacific Northwest Ballet 38
   Seattle Opera 38
McLaughlin, John 35
Me 'n' Moms 92
Meany Theatre 23
Medicinal Herb Garden 23
Mediterranean Inn, The 119
Mercer Island 55
Mercer Slough Nature Park 55
Mercer, Thomas 20
Merchant's Café and Saloon 15
Metropolitan Grill 50

Metropolitan Market 100
Metsker Maps of Seattle 69, 105
Meyer, Nancy 69
microbrews 49
Microsoft 23, 31, 42, 54
   code warriors 42
   Visitor Center 55
Mildred's B&B 117
Miller, Peter 69
Mishu Boutique 19
Mission 101
Moisture Festival 85
Montlake 20
Moore Hotel 118
Moore Theatre 38, 66
Moss Bay Rowing & Kayaking Center 45
Mount Rainier 13, 23, 58, 59
Mount Si 58
Mount St. Helens 58
Mt. Constitution 56
Mudhoney 48
Munter, Herb 30
Musashi's 51
Museum of Flight 37, 41
Museum of Glass 56
Museum of History & Industry 36
museums **36–37**
Myrtle Edwards Park 13

N
Naftaly, Bruce 51
Native American Roots 30
   Duwamish 30
   Muckleshoot 30
   Nisqually 30
   Snoqualmie 30
   Suquamish 30
Nectar Lounge 48
Neighbours 74
Neptune 39
Neumo's 49
nightlife **48–49**
Nirvana 66
Nisqually Earthquake 15, 31
Nordic Heritage Museum 89
Nordstrom 52, 65
Nordstrom, John W. 31, 52
Northern Exposure 57
Northern Pacific Railroad 30
Northwest African American Museum 37

Northwest Art & Frame 100
Northwest artists 37
Northwest Folklife Festival 35
Northwest Outdoor Center 45
Northwest Puppet Center 40
NW Film Forum 39

O
Ocean City 17
Old City Hall 56
Olmsted, John 24
Olympia 59
Olympic National Park 59
   Hurricane Ridge 59
Olympic Sculpture Park 13
Ophelia's Books 86
Other Coast Café, 91, 93

P
Pacific Place 52, 65
Pacific Science Center 11, 82
Pagdiriwang Philippine Festival 35
Panama Hotel 118
Paperhaus 68
Paramount Theatre 38
Paseo 87
Patagonia 68
Paul G. Allen Center for Computer Science & Engineering 23
PCC 83
Pendleton 69
Pensione Nichols 117
performing arts venues **38–39**
Pharmaca Integrative Pharmacy 100
Phil Smart 73
Phonecia 101
Pike Brewing Company 49
Pike Place Fish Company 8
Pike Place Market 6, **8–9**, 39, 43, 62, 89
   buskers 9
   Farmers Market 9
   Hillclimb 9
   underground mezzanines 8
Pike Street Fish Fry 77
Pill Hill 19
Pioneer Building 14, 33

Pioneer Square 6, **14–15**, 43, 61, 64
First Thursdays 15
Pioneer Square 15
Skid Road 15
waterfall garden 15
Place Pigalle 8
planning your trip **104**
Point Defiance Zoo & Aquarium 56
Ponti Seafood Grill 50
Port Townsend 57
Portland International Airport (PDX) 105
Presley, Elvis 11
Pretty Parlor 76
Pyramid Alehouse, Brewery & Restaurant 49

Q
Qazis 87
Queen City Grill 67
Quest Bookshop 18, 19, 76
Quinn's Pub 77

R
R Place 74
Rachel the Pig 9
Rainier Square 33, 53, 65
Rainier Tower 33, 53
Rancho Bravo Tacos 77
Rapunzel 81
Rautureau, Thierry 51
Ray's Boathouse & Café 50, 93
Re-Bar 74
re-souL 92
Red Door 87
Red Light 19
Redhook 49, 83
Redmond 31, 45, 55
REI 44, 45, 73
climbing rock walls 44
Remedy Teas 75
Renaissance Seattle 114
Rendezvous 66
Rendezvous Café/Jewel Box 39
renting gear 45
restaurants **50–51**
Richard Hugo House 72
Ride the Ducks 41
Ridgway, Gary 31
Robbins Brothers, The Engagement Ring Store 68

Rocket, The 84
Roosevelt Hotel, The 115
Roq La Rue Gallery 68
Roslyn 57
Ryan, Meg 21

S
Safeco Field 17
Saint Nicholas Russian Orthodox Cathedral 71
Salmon Bay Café 93
Salmon Bay Industries 91
Salty's on Alki Beach 99, 101
Sammamish River Trail 55
San Juan Islands 56
Sargent, John Singer 36
Scandinavian Specialties 92
Schmitz Preserve Park 46
Schultz, Howard 8, 31
Sea to Sky Rentals 119
Seafair & Tugboat Races 13, 34
Sealth, Chief 15, 30, 31, 9
Seattle Aquarium 12
Seattle Art Museum 36, 62
Hammering Man 36
Seattle Asian Art Museum 36, 46, 70, 72
Seattle Center 6, **10–11**, 34, 38
Center House 10
Seattle Center Monorail 11, 32, 64
Seattle Cherry Blossom & Japanese Cultural Festival 35
Seattle Children's Museum 10
Seattle Children's Theatre (SCT) 11
Seattle Chinese Garden 47
Seattle's Convention & Visitors Bureau 104
Seattle Gay News 109
Seattle Great Wheel 12, 65
Seattle Improvised Music Festival (SIMF) 35
Seattle International Film Festival (SIFF) 19, 35
Seattle Maritime Festival 34
Seattle Marriott Waterfront 41, 114
Seattle Metropolitan Police Museum 14

Seattle pastimes **42–43**
boating 43
gardening 42
Seattle Pride March 34, 72
Dykes on Bikes 34, 72
Seattle Post-Intelligencer 104
Seattle Storm 38
Seattle Suites 119
Seattle Times 104
Seattle Tower 33
Seattle Waterfront 6, **12–13**
Bell Harbor Marina 13
Cruise Ship Terminals 13
Olympic Sculpture Park 13
water sports & tours 13
Waterfront streetcar 12
Seattle's Best Coffee 42
Seattle's Best Tea 17
Seattle-Tacoma International Airport 17, 105
Second Ascent 45, 91
Secret Garden Bookshop 40, 92
security & health **111**
Sell Your Sole Consignment Boutique 68
Seven Stars Pepper Szechuan 16
Sexual Assault Hotline 111
Shafer Baillie Mansion 117
Sheraton Seattle 41, 114
Shiki Japanese Restaurant 51
Shilshole Bay 21, 45
Ship Canal Park 82
Shiro's 51
shopping tips **112**
Short-Term Suites 119
Show Pony 86
Showbox, The 48
shuttles 105
Silver Cloud Inn 41, 116
Simply Desserts 83
Six Arms 49
Skokomish River 59
Sky Church 39
Sleepless in Seattle 21
Smith Tower 14, 33
Smith, L.C. 14, 33
Snoqualmie Falls 58
Snoqualmie River 45
Sorrento Hotel 115
Soundgarden 48
South Seattle Community College 47

Space Needle 6, 10, 32, 41, 72
special needs **109**
Spirit of Washington 55
St. Mark's Episcopal Cathedral 71
staircase rapids 59
Starbucks 8, 42
  coffee 42
Statue of Liberty 99
Steinbrueck, Victor 8, 18, 39
Stone Gardens 44
  kayaking 44
stores & shopping centers **52–53**
Sub Pop World Headquarters 66
Summer Park Concerts 85
Sunday Farmers Market 90
Sunday Street Market 83
Sunset Tavern 49
Sushi restaurants 51
Suzzallo Library 23
Swallow's Nest Guest Cottages 117

T
Tacoma 30, 56
Tacoma Art Museum 56
Tacos Guaymas 87
Tavern Law 75
Tea House Kuan Yin 43
Têt Festival 35
Thanh Vi 16
Theo Chocolate 83
Three Girls Bakery 8
TibetFest 35
Tillicum Village 12, 13, 41
Tin Horse, The 53
Tobey, Mark 37
Tolt-MacDonald Park & Campground 45
Tonga Ridge 58
Top Pot Doughnuts 66
Top Ten Toys 40
toy stores 40
Tractor Tavern 48, 91
Traunfeld, Jerry 50
Travelex 110
Travelodge Seattle Center 41, 118
Triple Door, The 49
Tsue Chong Company Inc. 17
Tsutakawa, George 37
Tully's 42

Twin Falls 58
Two Bells Tavern 67

U
Uma 93
Uneeda Burger 87
Union Station 16
University District 20, 23
University District Street Fair 34
University Inn 41, 116
University Motel Suites 118
University of Washington 7, **22–23**, 34, 44, 47
  Red Square 22
  The Ave 23, 34
  The Hub 22
  University Book Store 23
University Village 52
Uptown Espresso & Bakery 10
urban retreats **46–47**
Uwajimaya 17

V
Vain 68
Vajra, The 19
Value Village 76
Varsity 39
Vashon Island 56, 97
Venkov, Emil 82
Via Tribunali 77
Victor Steinbrueck Park 8
Victoria, BC 57
Victrola Coffee 75
Volunteer Park 46, 70, 72
  Volunteer Park Conservatory 46, 72
  Volunteer Park Observation Tower 46, 72
Vuitton, Louis 53

W
W Seattle 115
Waiting for the Interurban 42, 81, 84
Walker, Milton 99
Walker Rock Garden 99
Wall of Sound 76
Wallingford Center 53
Walrus and the Carpenter, The 51, 93
Warwick Seattle 41, 118
Wasabi Bistro 51
Washington Park Arboretum & Japanese Garden 47

Washington State Convention Center 33, 53, 62
Washington State Ferries 12
Washington State History Museum 56
Waterfront Station 66
Watertown 116
West 5 101
West Point Lighthouse 26
West Seattle 56 **96–101**,
West Seattle Computers 100
  Dredging the Duwamish 98
  map 96
  places to eat 101
  shops 100
  steel mill 99
  The Junction 97
  West Seattle Bridge 97
Westfield Southcenter 53
Westin Seattle Hotel, The 41, 114
Westlake Center 52, 65
Weyerhaeuser, Frederick 30
Whale Museum 56
Wheel Fun Rentals 99, 106
Whidbey Island 56
Whiskey Bar 66
Whitebear, Bernie 27
Wildrose 74
Windworks Sailing Center 45
wineries 54
Wing Luke Museum 16, 37
Winslow 56
Winslow Homer 36
Woodland Park Rose Garden 46
Woodland Park Zoo 7, **24–25**, 46
  ZooTunes Summer Concerts 25
Wyeth, Andrew 36

Y
Yamasaki, Minoru 33
Ye Olde Curiosity Shop 13
Yesler, Henry 15, 30

Z
Zeitgeist 43

Acknowledgements

The Author
Eric Amrine is a freelance writer and musician living with his wife and two children in Seattle's Fremont district. His favorite travel assignments include hiking, kayaking, and wildlife, and have taken him through Alaska's Inside Passage via luxury yacht, white-water rafting in Oregon's Rogue River wilderness, and expedition cruising to pristine beaches and remote islands of the Sea of Cortez, Mexico.

Photographer Frank L. Jenkins
The photographer would like to thank Anna Webster for her assistance and help.

Additional Photography
Max Alexander, Andy Crawford, Philip Gatward, Heidi Grassley, Frank Greenaway, Dave King, Eddie Lawrence, Gunter Marx, Andrew McKinney, David Murray, Ian O'Leary, Scott Pitts, Guy Ryecart, Chris Stowers, Clive Streeter, David Sutton, Linda Whitwam, Francesca Yorke

AT DK INDIA:
Managing Editor Aruna Ghose
Art Editor Benu Joshi
Project Editor Vandana Bhagra
Project Designers Bonita Vaz, Divya Saxena
Senior Cartographer Uma Bhattacharya
Cartographer Alok Pathak
Picture Researcher Taiyaba Khatoon
Fact Checker Paul Townsend
Indexer & Proofreader Bhavna Seth Ranjan
DTP Co-ordinator Shailesh Sharma
DTP Designer Vinod Harish

AT DK LONDON:
Publishing Manager Helen Townsend
Managing Art Editor Jane Ewart
Senior Cartographic Editor Casper Morris
Senior DTP Designer Jason Little
DK Picture Library Romaine Werblow, Hayley Smith, Gemma Woodward
Production Linda Dare

Revisions Team
Ashwin Raju Adimari, Marta Bescos, Imogen Corke, Conrad van Dyk, Emer FitzGerald, Fay Franklin, Anna Freiberger, Rhiannon Furbear, Camilla Gersh, Eric Grossman, Katharina Hahn, Mohammad Hassan, Eric Houghton, Claire Jones, Priyanka Kumar, Rahul Kumar, Maite Lantaron, Hayley Maher, Nicola Malone, Alison McGill, Vikki Nousiainen, Sangita Patel, Carolyn Patten, Marianne Petrou, Marisa Renzullo, Erin Richards, Lucy Richards, Ellen Root, Farah Sheikh, Susana Smith, Nikky Twyman, Ajay Verma, Lisa Voormeij, Ros Walford

Picture Credits
Key: a-above; b-below/bottom; c-center; f-far; l-left; r-right; t-top.

The publisher would also like to thank the following for their assistance and kind permission to photograph at their establishments: Guitar Gallery at Experience Music Project, located in Seattle, Washington; Klondike Gold Rush National Historic Park; Pacific Place Shopping Center; Seattle Art Museum; Seattle Children's Museum; Smith Tower.

Works of art have been reproduced with the permission of the following copyright holders: Georgia Gerber *Rachel the Market Pig* 2tl, 62cl; Jonathan Borofsky *Hammering Man* 36ca; Seattle Public Utilities *Decorative Manhole Cover* 6bl; Jack Mackie *Dance Steps on Broadway* 1981 18b; Richard Beyer *People Waiting for the Interurban* 81b; Steve Badanes, Will Martin, Donna Walter and Ross Whitehead *Fremont Troll* 1990 82bl; Paul Sorey *Salmon Waves* 2001 89tr; Bill Garnett *West Seattle Ferries* 96c.

The publishers would like to thank the following individuals, companies and picture libraries for their kind permission to reproduce their photographs.

ALAMY: Brad Mitchell 4–5; Chuck Pefley 3bl, 21tl, 27tl, 76tl, 78–79; Robert Harding World Imagery 102–103; THE ART INSTITUTE OF SEATTLE: 66t.

BABELAND: Audrey McManus 74tc; THE BERGER PARTNERSHIP: The interactive water feature (sculpture) at Cal Anderson Park was a result of a collaborative effort between artist Doug Hollis and the landscape architect The Berger Partnership photo Doug Hollis 18–19.

CHAMBERED NAUTILUS BED & BREAKFAST INN: Jumping Rocks Photography 119tl; ANKUR CHOUBEY: 9crb, 69tl; CORBIS: Morton Beebe 34 tr; Richard Cummins 12–13c; Henry Diltz 31tr; Ric Ergenbright 22–23c; Kelly Mooney Photography 26–27c; Museum of History and Industry 30c; Douglas Peebles 6br, 35tr; Neil Rabinowitz 20–21c, 34tl, 34cl; Joel W. Rogers 9b; Museum of History and Industry/ © Seattle Post-Intelligencer Collection 37tr; Robert Sorbo 31tl; Paul A. Souders 60–61; Jay Syverson 16–17c; Karl Weatherly 28–29; Webster & Stevens Collection Seattle 30tl.

DAHLIA LOUNGE: 67tl; DREAMSTIME.COM: © Atleast1more 12c; DUSTY STRINGS: 86tl.

THE EDGEWATER HOTEL: 114tr.

FAIRMONT OLYMPIC HOTEL: 114tl.

GARAGE: Tom Marks Photo 77tl; GETTY IMAGES: Visions of America 9clb.

THE HERBFARM RESTAURANT: 51tl.

KUKURUZA GOURMET POPCORN: 92tr.

LOG HOUSE MUSEUM: 96tl; LUCCA GREAT FINDS: 92tl.

MANRAY VIDEO BAR: 74tr; MISHU BOUTIQUE: 19clb; THE MUSEUM OF FLIGHT: 41tl.

NANCY MEYER: 69tc.

OPHELIA'S BOOKS: 86tr.

PAPERHAUS: 68tr; PATAGONIA: 68tl; PETER MILLER: 69tr.

SEATTLE AQUARIUM: 6clb; SEATTLE ART MUSEUM: Richard Barnes 3br, 36tl; Benjamin Benschneider 13cr; SEATTLE CENTER: 10–11c; SEATTLE CONVENTION & VISITORS BUREAU: Daryl Smith *Jimi Hendrix Statue* photo David Blanchford 18tr; SEATTLE GREAT WHEEL: 62tr; SEATTLE PHOTOGRAPHS: Cherie Gates 14–15c; STA TRAVEL GROUP: 109tr.

TRIPLE DOOR THEATRE: 48bl.

WOODLAND PARK ZOO: Dennis Conner 24br, 25t, 24–25c, 25b.

All other images are © Dorling Kindersley. For further information see www.dkimages.com

Special Editions of DK Travel Guides

DK Travel Guides can be purchased in bulk quantities at discounted prices for use in promotions or as premiums. We are also able to offer special editions and personalized jackets, corporate imprints, and excerpts from all of our books, tailored specifically to meet your own needs.

To find out more, please contact:
(in the United States) **SpecialSales@dk.com**
(in the UK) **travelspecialsales@uk.dk.com**
(in Canada) DK Special Sales at **general@tourmaline.ca**
(in Australia) **business.development@pearson.com.au**

Selected Street Index

1st Avenue	H3
1st Avenue N	G2
2nd Avenue	H3
2nd Avenue N	H1
3rd Avenue	H3
3rd Avenue N	H1
4th Avenue	H3
4th Avenue N	H1
5th Avenue	H3
5th Avenue N	H1
6th Avenue	J3
6th Avenue N	J1
7th Avenue	J3
8th Avenue	J3
8th Avenue N	J2
9th Avenue	K3
9th Avenue N	J2
10th Avenue E	E3
10th Avenue W	C3
11th Avenue	M2
11th Avenue NE	E2
12th Avenue	M1
12th Avenue NE	E1
12th Avenue S	E5
13th Avenue	M1
14th Avenue	M1
15th Avenue E	E4
15th Avenue NE	E1
15th Avenue NW	C1
15th Avenue W	C3
19th Avenue	F5
20th Avenue E	F5
20th Avenue NW	B1
21st Avenue NE	F1
23rd Avenue W	B3
23rd Avenue S	F5
24th Avenue E	F4
24th Avenue NW	B1
25th Avenue NE	F1
28th Avenue NW	B1
28th Avenue W	B3
30th Avenue NW	B1
30th Avenue W	B3
32nd Avenue NW	B1
34th Avenue NW	B1
34th Street N	D3
35th Avenue NE	F2
35th Street N	D2
36th Avenue NW	B1
36th Avenue W	B3
36th Street N	D2
39th Street N	C2
40th Street N	D2
45th Street N	D2
45th Street NE	E2
47th Street N	E2
50th Street N	E2
60th Street NE	D1
60th Street NW	C1
63rd Avenue SW	A5
65th Street NE	F1
65th Street NW	C1
Admiral Way SW	A5
Alaska Street SW	A6
Alaskan Way	H3
Alder Street E	M5
Alki Avenue S	A5
Aloha Street	H1
Aloha Street E	L1
Armour Street W	B3
Aurora Avenue N	J2
Ballard Avenue	B1
Battery Street	H3
Beach Drive SW	A6
Bell Street	J3
Bellevue Avenue E	L1
Bellevue Place E	L1
Belmont Avenue E	L2
Belvoir Place	F2
Bertona Street W	A2
Blanchard Street	J3
Boat Street NE	E2
Boren Avenue	K3
Boren Avenue N	K2
Boston Street	D3
Boylston Avenue	L4
Boylston Avenue E	L2
Broad Street	H3
Broadway Avenue	M2
California Avenue SW	A5
Cedar Street	H3
Charles Street S	F6
Charlestown Street SW	A5
Cherry Street	K5
Cherry Street East	M4
Clay Street	H3
Columbia Street	K5
Columbia Street E	M4
Commodore Way	B2
Dearborn Street S	E6
Delmar Drive E	E3
Denny Way	H2
Denny Way E	L2
Dexter Avenue N	J1
Dravus Street West	B3
Eagle Street	G3
Eastlake Avenue E	L3
Eastlake Avenue N	L2
Elliott Avenue	H3
Elliott Avenue W	C4
Emerson Place W	B2
Fairview Avenue	K1
Fairview Avenue N	E3
Fauntleroy Way SW	B6
Fir Street E	M5
Fremont Avenue N	D2
Fuhrman Avenue	E2
Galer Street E	E4
Galer Street W	B3
Genesee Street SW	A5
Gilman Avenue W	B2
Gilman Drive W	C3
Government Way	B2
Green Lake Way NE	D1
Green Lake Way W	D1
Harbor Avenue SW	B2
Harrison Street	J2
Harrison Street E	M2
Harrison Street W	G2
Harvard Avenue E	L1
Holgate Street S	E6
Howell Street	K3
Howell Street E	L3
Jackson Street S	L6
James Street	K5
James Street E	L5
Jefferson Street E	M5
John Street	H2
John Street E	F4
John Street W	G2
King Street S	K6
Lake Washington Boulevard	F4
Lane Street S	L6
Latona Avenue NE	E1
Leary Avenue NW	B1
Leary Way NW	C2
Lenora Street	J3
Lynn Street	E3
Madison Street	K5
Madison Street E	F4
Magnolia Boulevard W	A3
Magnolia Bridge	B3
Main Street S	K6
Marion Street	K5
Marion Street E	M4
Market Street NW	B1
Martin Luther King Jr Way	F5
McGraw Street W	C3
Melrose Avenue E	L2
Mercer Street	G1
Mercer Street E	L1
Mercer Street W	D4
Meridian Avenue N	D2
Minor Avenue	L4
Minor Avenue N	K2
Montlake Boulevard N	F3
Morgan Street SW	B6
Nickerson Street W	D3
Olive Street E	L3
Olive Way	K3
Olive Way E	E4
Olympic Place W	C4
Pacific Street N	D2
Pacific Street NE	E2
Phinney Avenue N	D1
Pike Street	J4
Pike Street E	L3
Pine Street	J4
Pine Street E	L3
Pontius Avenue N	K1
Queen Ann Drive	C3
Queen Anne Avenue N	G1
Ravenna Boulevard	E1
Republican Street	H2
Republican Street E	L2
Republican Street W	G2
Roosevelt Way NE	E2
Roy Street	H1
Roy Street E	L1
Seaview Avenue NW	A1
Seneca Street	K5
Spring Street	H3
Spring Street E	M4
Spruce Street E	K5
Stewart Street	M5
Stewart Way	K3
Stone Way N	J4
Summit Avenue	D2
Summit Avenue E	L4
Terry Avenue	L2
Terry Avenue N	K3
Thomas Street	K2
Thomas Street E	H2
Thomas Street W	L2
Thorndyke Avenue W	G2
Union Bay Place NE	B3
Union Street	J4
Union Street E	L3
University Street	K4
University Way	E2
Valley Street	G1
Viewmont Way W	A3
Vine Street	H3
Virginia Street	J4
Wall Street	H3
Wallingford Avenue N	D2
Ward Street	K1
Warren Avenue N	G1
Washington Street S	K6
Weller Street S	L6
Western Avenue	H3
Westlake Avenue	J3
Westlake Avenue N	J2
Yale Avenue N	K1
Yesler Way	K5

Index